BANKING AND FINANCE

ECONOMICS

TAKING THE MYSTERY OUT OF MONEY

BANKING AND FINANCE

EDITED BY BRIAN DUIGNAN,
SENIOR EDITOR, RELIGION AND PHILOSOPHY

Britannica
Educational Publishing

IN ASSOCIATION WITH

ROSEN
EDUCATIONAL SERVICES

Published in 2013 by Britannica Educational Publishing
(a trademark of Encyclopædia Britannica, Inc.)
in association with Rosen Educational Services, LLC
29 East 21st Street, New York, NY 10010.

First Edition

Britannica Educational Publishing
J.E. Luebering: Senior Manager
Adam Augustyn: Assistant Manager
Marilyn L. Barton: Senior Coordinator, Production Control
Steven Bosco: Director, Editorial Technologies
Lisa S. Braucher: Senior Producer and Data Editor
Yvette Charboneau: Senior Copy Editor
Kathy Nakamura: Manager, Media Acquisition
Brian Duignan, Senior Editor, Religion and Philosophy

Rosen Educational Services
Nicholas Croce: Editor
Nelson Sá: Art Director
Cindy Reiman: Photography Manager
Marty Levick: Photo Researcher
Brian Garvey: Designer, Cover Design
Introduction by Richard Barrington

Library of Congress Cataloging-in-Publication Data

Banking and finance/edited by Brian Duignan.—1st ed.
   p. cm.—(Economics: taking the mystery out of money)
"In association with Britannica Educational Publishing, Rosen Educational Services"
Includes bibliographical references and index.
ISBN 978-1-61530-894-1 (library binding)
1. Banks and banking. 2. Finance. I. Duignan, Brian.
HG1601.B1727 2013
332.1—dc23

2012032631

Manufactured in the United States of America

Cover *Multi-bits/The Image Bank/Getty Images*; cover (background), pp. i, iii, 1, 11, 20, 33, 45,
63, 74, 89, 100 *zphoto/Shutterstock.com*

CONTENTS

7

18

21

96

98

INTRODUCTION

B anking and finance are typically thought of in numerical terms, such as dollars, interest rates, and loan amounts. This way of looking at these subjects may make them seem coldly mathematical. However, today's world of banking and finance includes so many varied elements, with such an intricate network of interdependence, that perhaps it can best be thought of as an ecosystem. Like an ecosystem, the environment of banking and finance can thrive on the interaction of different elements, but also like an ecosystem, there is always the danger that a problem in one area can quickly spread to other parts of the system.

This book will take you through the fundamental components of banking and finance to help you understand their components individually and see how they work together as part of a global financial system. That understanding will give you a better appreciation for the factors that often shape the economic headlines and the economy's future.

A good place to start in the study of banking and finance is with the definition of a bank. A bank is often described as a financial intermediary, which essentially means it is a form of middleman between people who have money to deposit and those who want to borrow money. This central principle—acting as an intermediary between depositors and borrowers—means that banks can lend and invest a far greater volume of money than their own capital because they have customer deposits available for those purposes.

There are various types of banks, but the two major categories are commercial banks and central banks. Commercial banks are privately owned, for-profit enterprises that do business with individuals and other businesses. Central banks are sponsored by national governments and conduct transactions primarily with commercial banks and other central banks. Central banks may also have responsibilities

for controling a nation's flow of money and for regulating the banking system.

One of the major roles that banks play in the economic system is to provide a substitute for hard currency. When someone writes a check or uses a debit card, balances are transferred electronically, which is much more convenient

Federal Reserve Chairman Ben Bernanke. Albert H. Teich/ Shutterstock.com than if money had to physically change hands. Providing bank money as a substitute for hard currency greatly facilitates commerce, but it also introduces an element of risk to the system, since at any given time banks hold only a small fraction of the total amount that has been deposited with them.

The reason that banks keep only a portion of their deposits on hand is that much of this money is being lent out to businesses and individuals. Providing credit in this way is another critical role that banks play in helping a modern economy operate and grow.

As traditional as these roles of banks are, they have evolved over time and continue to change. To provide some added perspective to modern banking and finance, this book will also cover some historical highlights. The history of banking can be traced back as far as ancient Mesopotamia. Much later, as trade and commerce grew substantially during the European Middle Ages, the role of banks grew as well, as banks provided loans, facilitated foreign exchange, and provided safekeeping of gold and silver.

Beginning in the 1500s, European banks evolved into two specialized types: exchange banks and deposit banks. While exchange banks, with their primary focus on facilitating foreign exchange, eventually faded in prominence compared to deposit banks, they were instrumental in establishing the concept of bank money, allowing for notional rather than physical transfers of money to facilitate trade. Another key part of this history is the introduction of banknotes, which evolved into the modern system of paper currency. Through these expanding roles, banks not only helped finance the spread of trade on a global scale but later also helped promote industrialization.

From these beginnings, banks evolved into their modern form. Though innovation continually adds new twists, the basic business model of a commercial bank is to pay customers interest for making deposits and charge them interest for taking out loans; much of the bank's profit comes from the difference between those interest rates. Those deposits are considered liabilities of the bank because they are amounts that must be paid to customers on demand; the loans are considered assets of the bank because they produce revenue. Managing the balance between assets and liabilities is the essence of bank risk management.

Banks use various techniques to manage this balance. They keep cash reserves on hand to repay a certain portion of deposits; they manage their assets by structuring a mix of short-term and long-term loans to provide a steady stream of liquidity; in most developed economies, banks also have access to a central bank, which can lend them money to cover temporary imbalances in their cash flows. In addition to managing assets, banks manage their liabilities with products such as certificates of deposit, which help them control the timing of customers' demands for their money.

Along with the challenge of coordinating the timing of assets and liabilities, banks also face credit and interest rate risk. As the risk environment has become more complex, banks have increasingly turned to sophisticated financial instruments, such as derivatives, to manage their risks. However, at times these instruments themselves have introduced a new element of risk to bank management. Because risk management is not perfect, bank capital serves as a cushion against asset losses and the demands of depositors. Bank capital is money put up by investors, who share in the profits earned by a bank but who are also the first to suffer losses when risk management fails.

Managing the risk of a bank, and of the banking system in general, is a complicated, high-stakes business. Bank regulators play the role of setting requirements for how this is handled and monitoring compliance with those requirements. This book will describe some of the critical issues in bank regulation. These issues include controls on how services are offered to the public, through the regulation of entry into the banking business and the establishment of branches, and restrictions on the rate of interest charged for loans. Regulators also attempt to ensure the financial soundness of banks through methods such as cash-reserve requirements and standards for the amount of capital banks must have.

While a system of independent commercial banks regulated by the government is the dominant banking model for most capitalist countries, this book also looks at the alternative of state-run or nationalized banks, which are common in socialist countries. This book also examines another significant aspect of government involvement in banking, which is the provision of deposit insurance.

While government typically plays only a regulatory role in commercial banking, its involvement in central banking is more hands-on. Central banks do not deal directly with the general public but rather serve as a banking resource for commercial banks and the government. They perform basic functions such as serving as a source of currency, as well as more complex functions such as attempting to moderate inflation and economic cycles.

Some of the functions performed by today's central banks can be traced back to European public or municipal banks in the 15th century. The Bank of England, founded in 1694, became particularly influential in shaping the role of the modern central bank. In the United States, the Federal Reserve System was established as the nation's central bank in 1913, and in the early part of the 20th century the central banking system became the norm for the world's developed economies.

This book will follow the development of central banks into their modern role, which has become tremendously influential in the regulation of currency flows, the stability of the banking system, and the implementation of national economic policies. While central banks don't do business with the public directly, their functions are likely to influence the strength of the economy you live and work in, the rate of inflation on the goods you buy, and the interest rate you pay when you take out a loan.

The importance of central banks will be illustrated by looking at some prominent examples of central banks and discussing how their roles continue to evolve as financial institutions become ever more complex. The global nature of economics and banking became such that the World Bank, which is associated with the United Nations, was formed in 1944 to help promote economic development around the world. Though the World Bank is different in organization and function from a central bank, it plays a somewhat complementary role on a global scale, and the description of the World Bank's history and policies will help complete the picture of how the diverse banking activities of individuals and businesses are formally coordinated.

At both the individual-bank level and the level of coordinating institutions such as central banks and the World Bank, the role of banks is essential to the financial activities of large and small businesses alike. The latter part of this book will look at some of the essentials of business finance, in terms of both short-term transactions and long-term structure and growth.

Managing the finances of a business is usually the responsibility of a senior member of the organization, with this role being more formalized—and involving a staff of specialists—in larger companies. Goals of this job include ensuring operational solvency, making the most of a firm's resources, and budgeting. A key tool in this effort is financial ratio analysis, which helps ensure that the diverse elements of a firm's balance sheet and cash flow are in proper proportion to each other. These activities help facilitate a firm's current operations, but financial managers also play a role in determining a company's future plans through profit planning and financial forecasting.

The structure on which an organization's finances are based is a budget, and by examining the elements of a corporate budget this book will give you a feel for some of the nuts and bolts of corporate finance. Budgets help regulate the flow of cash into and out of a company—too little cash on hand can interrupt operations or cause a company to seek additional financing, while too much cash can mean that resources are not being put to productive use. By extension, budgets also help manage elements that affect cash flow, such as accounts receivable and inventories.

Where does banking enter into this process of corporate finance? As a practical matter, it is not always possible to have cash from normal operations on hand to pay for each new expenditure, especially when it comes to expansion or other new investments. Banks help provide this liquidity in the form of short and intermediate loans. However, banks cannot always provide the best solution for a company's needs, so this book will also look at other forms of financing, such as commercial paper, conditional sales contracts, and leasing.

These short- and intermediate-term financing systems work well in the context of normal operations and incremental growth, but for a company to grow to the scale of General Motors Corporation or Apple Inc., a more robust form of financing is required. Long-term financing programs are necessary to fund such large-scale operations and make massive investments in the future.

Major long-term financing options include selling bonds and issuing stock. Selling bonds is a way of borrowing money, but the debt is sold publicly rather than arranged through a private lender. Issuing stock allows a company to avoid taking on debt, but it means giving up a share of future profits to the stockholders. There are also hybrid forms of financing to consider, such as convertible bonds and stock warrants, which can incorporate elements of both stocks and bonds.

Choosing the right mix of stock and bond usage is one of the critical decisions in corporate finance. It can make a difference of millions or even billions of dollars to a company's founders, and it can also mean the difference between survival and bankruptcy. Sometimes, the best path to growth might lead through merger with another company; in other cases, survival may depend on a fundamental reorganization of the company.

This world of corporate finance may seem far-removed from most people's experience, something that takes place high up in corporate boardrooms. However, in shaping the future of both large and small businesses, corporate finance has the power to create the products and jobs that affect people from all walks of life. Together with the banking system, corporate finance is critical to the economic ecosystem in which we exist.

CHAPTER ONE

PRINCIPLES OF BANKING

A bank is an institution that deals in money and its substitutes and provides other money-related services. In its role as a financial intermediary, a bank accepts deposits and makes loans. It derives a profit from the difference between the costs (including interest payments) of attracting and servicing deposits and the income it receives through interest charged to borrowers or earned through securities (investment instruments, such as stocks and bonds, that entitle their bearers to receive certain kinds of property). Many banks provide related services such as financial management and products such as mutual funds and credit cards. Some bank liabilities also serve as money—that is, as generally accepted means of payment and exchange.

The central practice of banking consists of borrowing and lending. As in other businesses, operations must be based on capital, but banks employ comparatively little of their own capital in relation to the total volume of their transactions. Instead, banks use the funds obtained through deposits and, as a precaution, maintain capital and reserve accounts to protect against losses on their loans and investments and to provide for unanticipated cash withdrawals. Genuine banks are distinguished from other kinds of financial intermediaries by the readily transferable or "spendable" nature of at least some of their liabilities (also known as IOUs), which allows those liabilities to serve as means of exchange—that is, as money.

TYPES OF BANKS

The principal types of banks in the modern industrial world are commercial banks, which are typically private-sector profit-oriented firms, and central banks, which are public-sector institutions. Commercial banks accept deposits from the general public and make various kinds of loans (including commercial, consumer, and real-estate loans) to individuals and businesses and, in some instances, to governments. Central banks, in contrast, deal mainly with their sponsoring national governments, with commercial banks, and with each other. Besides accepting deposits from and extending credit to these clients, central banks also issue paper currency and are responsible for regulating commercial banks and national money stocks.

The term *commercial bank* covers institutions ranging from small neighbourhood banks to huge metropolitan institutions or multinational organizations with hundreds of branches. Although U.S. banking regulations limited the development of nationwide bank chains through most of the 20th century, legislation in 1994 easing these limitations led American commercial banks to organize along the lines of their European counterparts, which typically operated offices and bank branches in many regions.

In the United States a distinction exists between commercial banks and so-called thrift institutions, which include savings and loan associations (S&Ls), credit unions, and savings banks. Like commercial banks, thrift institutions accept deposits and fund loans, but unlike commercial banks, thrifts have traditionally

Citibank is the commercial banking branch of Citigroup, one of the largest financial services conglomerates in the world. Emmanuel Dunand/AFP/Getty Images

FINANCE COMPANY

Finance companies are specialized financial institutions that supply credit for the purchase of consumer goods and services by purchasing the time-sales contracts of merchants or by granting small loans directly to consumers. Specialized consumer-finance agencies operate throughout western Europe, Canada, the United States, Australia, Japan, and some Latin American countries. Although they existed in the early 1900s, their greatest development came after World War II.

Large-sales finance companies, which operate by purchasing unpaid customer accounts at a discount from merchants and collecting payments due from consumers, were a response to the need for installment financing for the purchase of automobiles in the early 1900s. The General Motors Acceptance Corporation (now Ally Financial), for example, was established in 1919 to purchase automobile accounts receivable from car dealers who were themselves unable to finance time purchases. Many companies in both Europe and the United States continue to specialize in financing purchases of particular commodities and remain closely associated with specific manufacturers. Some also extend credit for wholesale purchases by retail dealers. Consumer finance or small-loan companies also arose in the 1900s. Until then, the need for consumer loans had been met primarily by illegal "loan shark" activities because it was unprofitable for banks to make small loans at rates below legally set usury levels. In 1911 several states in the United States began adopting small-loan laws that authorized loans to consumers at rates above usury levels, making it financially practical to operate a consumer-loan business. Today many companies engage both in the sales-finance business and in making loans directly to consumers.

In some countries, including Belgium, Denmark, and Norway, commercial banks have also become important as a direct source of consumer credit. In many other countries, they are important as a source of capital for specialized finance companies. Many finance companies in Great Britain, Australia, and the Netherlands, for example, have become closely affiliated with commercial banks because of the banks' role as capital subscribers. In other cases, commercial banks play an important role in their extension of credit to finance companies.

focused on residential mortgage lending rather than commercial lending. The growth of a separate thrift industry in the United States was largely fostered by regulations unique to that country; these banks therefore lack a counterpart elsewhere in the world. Moreover, their influence has waned: the pervasive deregulation of American commercial banks, which originated in the wake of S&L failures during the late 1980s, weakened the competitiveness of such banks and left the future of the U.S. thrift industry in doubt.

While these and other institutions are often called banks, they do not perform all the banking functions described above and are best classified as financial intermediaries. Institutions that fall into this category include finance companies, savings banks, investment banks (which deal primarily with large business clients and are mainly concerned with underwriting and distributing new issues of corporate bonds and equity shares), trust companies, finance companies (which specialize in making risky loans and do not accept deposits), insurance companies, mutual fund companies, and home-loan banks or savings and loan associations. One particular type of commercial bank, the merchant bank (known as an investment bank in the United States), engages in investment banking activities such as advising on mergers and acquisitions. In some countries, including Germany, Switzerland, France, and Italy, so-called universal banks supply both traditional (or "narrow") commercial banking services and various nonbank financial services such as securities underwriting and insurance. Elsewhere, regulations, long-established custom, or a combination of both have limited the extent to which commercial banks have taken part in the provision of nonbank financial services.

BANK MONEY

The development of trade and commerce drove the need for readily exchangeable forms of money. The concept of bank money originated with the Amsterdamsche Wisselbank (the Bank of Amsterdam), which was established in 1609 during Amsterdam's ascent as the largest and most prosperous city in Europe. As an exchange bank, it permitted individuals to bring money or bullion for deposit and to withdraw the money or the worth of the bullion. The original ordinance that established the bank further required that all bills of 600 gulden or upward should be paid through the bank—in other words, by the transfer of deposits or credits at the bank. These transfers later came to be known as "bank money." The charge for making the transfers represented the bank's sole source of income.

In contrast to the earliest forms of money, which were commodity moneys based on items such as seashells, tobacco, and precious-metal coin, practically all contemporary money takes the form of bank money, which

A 17th-century oil painting of Amsterdamsche Wisselbank by Pieter Saenredam. G. Dalgi Orti/De Agostini Picture Library/Getty Images

consists of checks or drafts that function as commercial or central bank IOUs. Commercial bank money consists mainly of deposit balances that can be transferred either by means of paper orders (e.g., checks) or electronically (e.g., debit cards, wire transfers, and Internet payments). Some electronic-payment systems are equipped to handle transactions in a number of currencies.

Circulating "banknotes," yet another kind of commercial bank money, are direct claims against the issuing institution (rather than claims to any specific depositor's account balance). They function as promissory notes issued by a bank and are payable to a bearer on demand without interest, which makes them roughly equivalent to money. Although their use was widespread before the 20th century, banknotes have been replaced largely by transferable bank deposits. In the early 21st century only a handful of commercial banks issued banknotes. For the most part, contemporary paper currency consists of fiat money (from the medieval Latin term meaning "let it be done"), which is issued by central banks or other public monetary authorities.

All past and present forms of commercial bank money share the characteristic of being redeemable (that is, freely convertible at a fixed rate) in some under-lying base money, such as fiat money (as is the case in contemporary banking) or a commodity money such as gold or silver coin. Bank customers are effectively guaranteed the right to seek unlimited redemptions of commercial bank money on demand (that is, without delay); any commercial bank refusing to honour the obligation to redeem its bank money is typically deemed insolvent. The same rule applies to the routine redemp-tion requests that a bank makes, on behalf of its clients, upon another bank—as when a check drawn upon Bank A is presented to Bank B for collection.

While commercial banks remain the most impor-tant sources of convenient substitutes for base money, they are no longer exclusive suppliers of money substi-tutes. Money-market mutual funds and credit unions offer widely used money substitutes by permitting the persons who own shares in them to write checks from their accounts. (Money-market funds and credit unions differ from commercial banks in that they are owned by and lend only to their own depositors.) Another money substitute, traveler's checks, resembles old-fashioned banknotes to some degree, but they must be endorsed by their users and can be used for a single transaction only, after which they are redeemed and retired.

For all the efficiencies that bank money brings to financial transactions and the marketplace, a heavy reliance upon it—and upon spendable bank deposits in particular—can expose economies to banking crises. This is because banks hold only fractional reserves of basic money, and any concerted redemption of a bank's deposits—which could occur if the bank is suspected of insolvency—can cause it to fail. On a larger scale, any concerted redemption of a country's bank deposits (assuming the withdrawn funds are not simply redeposited in other banks) can altogether destroy an economy's banking system, depriving it of needed means of exchange as well as of business and consumer credit. Perhaps the most notorious example of this was the U.S. banking crisis of the early 1930s.

BANK LOANS

Bank loans, which are available to businesses of all types and sizes, represent one of the most important sources of commercial funding throughout the industrialized world. Key sources of funding for corporations include loans, stock and bond issues, and income. In the United States, for example, the funding that business enterprises obtain from banks is roughly twice the amount they receive by marketing their own bonds, and funding from bank loans is far greater still than what companies acquire by issuing shares of stock. In Germany and Japan bank loans represent an even larger share of total business funding. Smaller and more specialized sources of funding include venture capital firms and hedge funds.

Direct-to-consumer loans allow virtually anyone with acceptable credit to finance big-ticket items such as automobiles. Justin Sullivan/Getty Images

Although all banks make loans, their lending practices differ, depending on the areas in which they specialize. Commercial loans, which can cover time frames ranging from a few weeks to a decade or more, are made to all kinds of businesses and represent a very important part of commercial banking worldwide. Some commercial banks devote an even greater share of their lending to real-estate financing (through mortgages and home-equity loans) or to direct consumer loans (such as personal and automobile loans). Others specialize in particular areas, such as agricultural loans or construction loans. As a general business practice, most banks do not restrict themselves to lending but acquire and hold other assets, such as government and corporate securities and foreign exchange (that is, cash or securities denominated in foreign currency units).

CHAPTER TWO

HISTORICAL DEVELOPMENT

Some authorities, relying upon a broad definition of banking that equates it with any sort of intermediation activity, trace banking as far back as ancient Mesopotamia, where temples, royal palaces, and some private houses served as storage facilities for valuable commodities such as grain, the ownership of which could be transferred by means of written receipts. There are records of loans by the temples of Babylon as early as 2000 BCE; temples were considered especially safe depositories because, as they were sacred places watched over by gods, their contents were believed to be protected from theft. Companies of traders in ancient times

Mesopotamian temples such as the Ziggurat of Ur are believed to have been the depositories used in early banking. Peter Visscher/Getty Images

provided banking services that were connected with the buying and selling of goods. Many of these early "proto-banks" dealt primarily in coin and bullion, much of their business being money changing and the supplying of foreign and domestic coin of the correct weight and fineness.

EARLY EUROPEAN BANKING

Full-fledged banks did not emerge until medieval times, with the formation of organizations specializing in the depositing and lending of money and the creation of generally spendable IOUs that could serve in place of coins or other commodity moneys. In Europe so-called "merchant bankers" paralleled the development of banking by offering, for a consideration, to assist merchants in making distant payments, using bills of exchange instead of actual coin. The merchant banking business arose from the fact that many merchants traded internationally, holding assets at different points along trade routes. For a certain consideration, a merchant stood prepared to accept instructions to pay money to a named party through one of his agents elsewhere; the amount of the bill of exchange would be debited by his agent to the account of the merchant banker, who would also hope to make an additional profit from exchanging one currency against another. Because there was a possibility of loss, any profit or gain was not subject to the medieval ban on usury. There were, moreover, techniques for concealing a loan by making foreign exchange available at a distance but deferring payment for it so that the interest charge could be camouflaged as a fluctuation in the exchange rate.

The earliest genuine European banks, in contrast, dealt neither in goods nor in bills of exchange but in gold and silver coins and bullion, and they emerged in response to the risks involved in storing and transporting precious metal moneys and, often, in response to the deplorable quality of available coins, which created a demand for more reliable and uniform substitutes.

In continental Europe dealers in foreign coin, or "money changers," were among the first to offer basic banking services, while in London money "scriveners" and goldsmiths played a similar role. Money scriveners were notaries who found themselves well positioned for bringing borrowers and lenders together, while goldsmiths began their transition to banking by keeping money and valuables in safe custody for their customers. Goldsmiths also dealt in bullion and foreign exchange, acquiring and sorting coin for profit. As a means of attracting coin for sorting, they were prepared to pay a rate of interest, and it was largely in this way that they eventually began to outcompete money scriveners as deposit bankers.

SPECIALIZATION

Banks in Europe from the 16th century onward could be divided into two classes: exchange banks and banks of deposit. The last were banks that, besides receiving deposits, made loans and thus associated themselves with the trade and industries of a country. The exchange banks included in former years institutions such as the Bank of Hamburg and the Bank of Amsterdam. These were established to deal with foreign exchange and to facilitate trade with other countries. The others—founded at very different dates—were established as, or early became, banks of deposit, such as the Bank of England, the Bank of Venice, the Bank of Sweden, the Bank of France, the Bank of Germany, and others. Important as exchange banks were in their day, the period of their activity had generally passed by the last half of the 19th century.

In one particularly notable respect, the business carried on by the exchange banks differed from banking as generally understood at the time. Exchange banks were established for the primary purpose of turning the values with which they were entrusted into bank money—that is, into a currency that merchants accepted immediately, with no need to test the value of the coin or the bullion given to them. The value the banks provided was equal to the value they received, with the only difference being the small amount charged to their customers for performing such transactions. No exchange bank had capital of its own, nor did it require any for the performance of its business.

In every case, deposit banking at first involved little more than the receipt of coins for safekeeping or warehousing, for which service depositors were required to pay a fee. By early modern times this warehousing

The use of physical checks today is just one method in a long history of ways of transacting money between parties. Thomas M. Perkins/Shutterstock.com

function had given way in most cases to genuine inter-mediation, with deposits becoming debt as opposed to bailment (delivery in trust) contracts, and depositors sharing in bank interest earnings instead of paying fees. Concurrent with this change was the development of bank money, which had begun with transfers of deposit credits by means of oral and later written instructions to bankers and also with the endorsement and assign-ment of written deposit receipts; each transaction presupposed legal acknowledgement of the fungible (interchangeable) status of deposited coins. Over time, deposit transfers by means of written instructions led directly to modern checks.

THE DEVELOPMENT OF BANKNOTES

Although the Bank of England is usually credited with being the source of the Western world's first widely circulated banknotes, the Stockholms Banco (Bank of Stockholm, founded in 1656 and the predecessor of the contemporary Bank of Sweden) is known to have issued banknotes several decades before the Bank of England's establishment in 1694, and some authori-ties claim that notes issued by the Casa di San Giorgio (Bank of Genoa, established in 1407), although pay-able only to specific persons, were made to circulate by means of repeated endorsements. In Asia, paper money has a still longer history, its first documented use having been in China during the 9th century, when "flying money"—a sort of draft or bill of exchange developed by merchants—was gradually transformed

LAW OF LARGE NUMBERS

The law of large numbers is a theorem in statistics. It states that, as the number of identically distributed, randomly generated variables increases, their sample mean (average) approaches their theoretical mean.

The law of large numbers was first proved by the Swiss mathematician Jakob Bernoulli in 1713. He and his contemporaries were developing a formal probability theory with a view toward analyzing games of chance. Bernoulli envisaged an endless sequence of repetitions of a game of pure chance with only two outcomes, a win or a loss. Labeling the probability of a win p, Bernoulli considered the fraction of times that such a game would be won in a large number of repetitions. It was commonly believed that this fraction should eventually be close to p. This is what Bernoulli proved in a precise manner by showing that, as the number of repetitions increases indefinitely, the probability of this fraction being within any prespecified distance from p approaches 1.

There is also a more general version of the law of large numbers for averages, proved more than a century later by the Russian mathematician Pafnuty Chebyshev.

The law of large numbers is closely related to what is commonly called the law of averages. In coin tossing, the law of large numbers stipulates that the fraction of heads will eventually be close to ½. Hence, if the first 10 tosses produce only 3 heads, it seems that some mystical force must somehow increase the probability of a head, producing a return of the fraction of heads to its ultimate limit of ½. Yet the law of large numbers requires no such mystical force. Indeed, the fraction of heads can take a very long time to approach ½. For example, to obtain a 95 percent probability that the fraction of heads falls between 0.47 and 0.53, the number of tosses must exceed 1,000. In other words, after 1,000 tosses, an initial shortfall of only 3 heads out of 10 tosses is swamped by results of the remaining 990 tosses.

into government-issued fiat money. The 12th-century Tatar war caused the government to abuse this new financial instrument, and China thereby earned credit not merely for the world's first paper money but also for the world's first known episode of hyperinflation. Several more such episodes caused the Chinese government to cease issuing paper currency, leaving the matter to private bankers. By the late 19th century, China had developed a unique and, according to many accounts, successful bank money system, consisting of paper notes issued by unregulated local banks and redeemable in copper coin. Yet the system was undermined in the early 20th century, first by demands made by the government upon the banks and ultimately by the decision to centralize and nationalize China's paper currency system.

The development of bank money increased bankers' ability to extend credit by limiting occasions when their clients would feel the need to withdraw currency. The increasingly widespread use of bank money eventually allowed bankers to exploit the law of large numbers, whereby withdrawals would be offset by new deposits. Market competition, however, prevented banks from extending credit beyond reasonable means, and each bank set aside cash reserves, not merely to cover occasional coin withdrawals but also to settle interbank accounts. Bankers generally found it to be in their interest to receive, on deposit, checks drawn upon or notes

Illustration of a clearinghouse in London, England, circa 1830.
Hulton Archive/Getty Images

issued by rivals in good standing; it became a standard practice for such notes or checks to be cleared (that is, returned to their sources) on a routine (usually daily) basis, where the net amounts due would be settled in coin or bullion. Starting in the late 18th century, bankers found that they could further economize on cash reserves by setting up clearinghouses in major cities to manage nonlocal bank money clearings and settlements, as doing so allowed further advantage to be taken of opportunities for "netting out" offsetting items, that is, offsetting gross credits with gross debits, leaving net dues alone to be settled with specie (coin money). Clearinghouses were the precursors to contemporary institutions such as clearing banks, automated clearinghouses, and the Bank for International Settlements. Other financial innovations, such as the development of bailment and bank money, created efficiencies in transactions that complemented the process of industrialization. In fact, many economists, starting with the Scottish philosopher Adam Smith, have attributed to banks a crucial role in promoting industrialization.

CHAPTER THREE

COMMERCIAL BANKING

The essential business of banking involves granting bank deposit credits or issuing IOUs in exchange for deposits (which are claims to base money, such as coins or fiat paper money); banks then use the base money—or that part of it not needed as cash reserves—to purchase other IOUs with the goal of earning a profit on that investment. The business may be most readily understood by considering the elements of a simplified bank balance sheet, where a bank's available resources—its "assets"—are reckoned alongside its obligations, or "liabilities."

ASSETS

Bank assets consist mainly of various kinds of loans and marketable securities and of reserves of base money, which may be held either as actual central banknotes and coins or in the form of a credit (deposit) balance at the central bank. The bank's main liabilities are its capital (including cash reserves and, often, subordinated debt) and deposits. The latter may be from domestic or foreign sources (corporations and firms, private individuals, other banks, and even governments). They may be repayable on demand (sight deposits or current accounts) or after a period of time (time, term, or fixed deposits and, occasionally, savings deposits). The bank's assets include cash; investments or securities; loans and advances made to customers of all kinds, though primarily to corporations (including term loans and mortgages); and, finally, the bank's premises, furniture, and fittings.

Though transactions are often done electronically, banks' deposits are still secured in physical form in vaults. iStockphoto/Thinkstock

The difference between the fair market value of a bank's assets and the book value of its outstanding liabilities represents the bank's net worth. A bank lacking positive net worth is said to be "insolvent," and it generally cannot remain open unless it is kept afloat by means of central bank support. At all times a bank must maintain cash balances to pay its depositors upon demand. It must also keep a proportion of its assets in forms that can readily be converted into cash. Only in this way can confidence in the banking system be maintained.

The main resource of a modern bank is borrowed money (that is, deposits), which the bank loans out as profitably as is prudent. Banks also hold cash reserves for interbank settlements as well as to provide depositors with cash on demand, thereby maintaining a "safe" ratio of cash to deposits. The safe cash-to-assets ratio may be established by convention or by statute. If a minimum cash ratio is required by law, a portion of a bank's assets is in effect frozen and not available to meet sudden demands for cash from the bank's customers (though the requirement can be enforced in such a way as to allow banks to dip into required reserves on occasion—e.g., by substituting "lagged" for "contemporaneous" reserve accounting). To provide more flexibility, required ratios are frequently based on the average of cash holdings over a specified period, such as a week or a month.

Unless a bank held cash equivalent to 100 percent of its demand deposits, it could not meet the claims of depositors were they all to exercise in full and at the same time their right to demand cash. If that were a common phenomenon, deposit banking could not survive. For the most part, however, the public is prepared to leave its surplus funds on deposit with banks, confident that money will be available when needed. But there may be times when unexpected demands for cash exceed what might reasonably have been anticipated; therefore, a bank must not only hold part of its assets in cash but also must keep a proportion of the remainder in assets that can be quickly converted into cash without significant loss.

ASSET MANAGEMENT

A bank may mobilize its assets in several ways. It may demand repayment of loans, immediately or at short notice; it may sell securities; or it may borrow from the central bank, using paper representing investments or loans as security. Banks do not precipitately call in loans or sell marketable assets because this would disrupt the delicate debtor-creditor relationship and lessen confidence, which probably would result in a run on the banks. Banks therefore maintain cash reserves and other liquid assets at a certain level or have access to a "lender of last resort," such as a central bank. In a number of countries, commercial banks have at times been required to maintain a minimum liquid assets ratio. Among the assets of commercial banks, investments are less liquid than money-market assets. By maintaining an appropriate spread of maturities (through a combination of long-term and short-term investments), however, it is possible to ensure that a proportion of a bank's investments will regularly approach redemption. This produces a steady flow of liquidity and thereby constitutes a secondary liquid assets reserve.

Yet this necessity—to convert a significant portion of its liabilities into cash on demand—forces banks to "borrow short and lend long." Because most bank loans have definite maturity dates, banks must exchange IOUs that may be redeemed at any time for IOUs that will not come due until some definite future date. That makes even the most solvent banks subject to liquidity risk— that is, the risk of not having enough cash (base money) on hand to meet demands for immediate payment.

Banks manage this liquidity risk in a number of ways. One approach, known as asset management, concentrates on adjusting the composition of the bank's assets—its portfolio of loans, securities, and cash. This approach exerts little control over the bank's liabilities and overall size, both of which depend on the number of customers who deposit savings in the bank. In general, bank managers build a portfolio of assets capable of earning the greatest interest revenue possible while keeping risks within acceptable bounds. Bankers must also set aside cash reserves sufficient to meet routine demands (including the demand for reserves to meet minimum statutory requirements) while devoting remaining funds mainly to short-term commercial loans. The presence of many short-term loans among a bank's assets means that some bank loans are always coming due, making it possible for a bank to meet exceptional cash withdrawals or settlement dues by refraining from renewing or replacing some maturing loans.

The practice among early bankers of focusing on short-term commercial loans, which was understandable given the assets they had to choose from, eventually became the basis for a fallacious theory known as the "real bills doctrine," according to which there could be no risk of banks overextending themselves or generating inflation as long as they stuck to short-term lending, especially if they limited themselves to discounting commercial bills or promissory notes supposedly representing "real" goods in various stages of production. The

Commercial loans are often the only means by which businesses can purchase expensive equipment, such as heavy machinery, to conduct business. iStockphoto/Thinkstock

TREASURY BILL

A treasury bill is a short-term U.S. government security with maturity ranging from four weeks to 52 weeks. Treasury bills are usually sold at auction on a discount basis with a yield equal to the difference between the purchase price and the maturity value. In contrast to longer-term government securities, such as treasury notes (with maturity ranging between 1 and 10 years), treasury bills are much more liquid investments (i.e., cash for alternative investments is tied up for shorter periods of time). Because of this high liquidity, the yield rate on treasury bills is normally lower than on longer-term securities. Prices of treasury bills do not usually fluctuate as much as those of other government securities but may be influenced by the purchase or sale of large quantities of bills by the central bank. From 1970 to 1998 the minimum order for treasury bills was $10,000, after which it was reduced to $1,000 and then to $100.

First used extensively during World War I and initially regarded as an emergency source of revenue, bills and other short-term debt instruments have become a permanent element in the public debt of several countries because of their relatively low-interest cost and greater flexibility. Treasury bills are ordinarily held as secondary reserves by commercial banks and by other investors as a means of temporarily employing excess funds.

real bills doctrine erred in treating both the total value of outstanding commercial bills and the proportion of such bills presented to banks for discounting as being values independent of banking policy (and independent of bank discount and interest rates in particular). According to the real bills doctrine, if such rates are set low enough, the volume of loans and discounts will increase while the outstanding quantity of bank money will expand; in turn, this expansion may cause the general price level to rise. As prices rise, the nominal stock of "real bills" will tend to grow as well. Inflation might therefore continue forever despite strict adherence by banks to the real bills rule.

Although the real bills doctrine continues to command a small following among some contemporary economists, by the late 19th century most bankers had abandoned the practice of limiting themselves to short-term commercial loans, preferring instead to mix such loans with higher-yielding long-term investments. This change stemmed in part from increased transparency and greater efficiency in the market for long-term securities. These improvements have made it easy for an individual bank to find buyers for such securities whenever it seeks to exchange them for cash. Banks also have made greater use of money-market assets such as treasury bills, which combine short maturities with ready marketability and are a favoured form of collateral for central bank loans.

Commercial banks in some countries, including Germany, also make long-term loans to industry (also known as commercial loans) despite the fact that such loans are neither self-liquidating (capable of generating cash) nor readily marketable. These banks must ensure their liquidity by maintaining relatively high levels of capital (including conservatively valued shares in the enterprises they are helping to fund) and by relying more heavily on longer-term borrowings (including time deposits as well as the issuance of bonds or unsecured debt, such as debentures). In other countries, including Japan and the United States, long-term corporate financing is handled primarily by financial institutions that specialize in commercial loans and securities underwriting rather than by banks.

LIABILITY AND RISK MANAGEMENT

The traditional asset management approach to banking is based on the assumption that a bank's liabilities are both relatively stable and unmarketable. Historically, each bank relied on a market for its deposit IOUs that was influenced by the bank's location, meaning that any changes in the extent of the market (and hence in the total amount of resources available to fund the bank's loans and investments) were beyond a bank's immediate control. In the 1960s and '70s, however, this assumption was abandoned. The change occurred first in the United States, where rising interest rates, together with regulations limiting the interest rates banks could pay, made it increasingly difficult for banks to attract and maintain deposits. Consequently, bankers devised a variety of alternative devices for acquiring funds, including repurchase agreements, which involve the selling of securities on the condition that buyers agree to repurchase them at a stated date in the future, and negotiable certificates of deposit (CDs), which can be traded in a secondary market. Having discovered new ways to acquire funds, banks no longer waited for funds to arrive through the normal course of business. The new approaches enabled banks to manage the liability as well as the asset side of their balance sheets. Such active purchasing and selling of funds by banks, known as liability management, allows bankers to exploit profitable lending opportunities without being limited by a lack of funds for loans. Once liability management became an established practice in the United States, it quickly spread to Canada and the United Kingdom and eventually to banking systems worldwide.

A more recent approach to bank management synthesizes the asset- and liability-management approaches. Known as risk management, this approach essentially treats banks as bundles of risks; the primary challenge for bank managers is to establish acceptable degrees of risk exposure. This means bank managers must calculate a reasonably reliable measure of their bank's overall exposure to various risks and then adjust the bank's portfolio to achieve both an acceptable overall risk level and the greatest shareholder value consistent with that level.

Contemporary banks face a wide variety of risks. In addition to liquidity risk, they include credit risk (the risk that borrowers will fail to repay their loans on schedule), interest-rate risk (the risk that market interest rates will rise relative to rates being earned on outstanding long-term loans), market risk (the risk of suffering losses in connection with asset and liability trading), foreign-exchange risk (the risk of a foreign currency in which loans have been made being devalued during the loans' duration), and sovereign risk (the risk that a government will default on its debt). The risk-management approach differs from earlier approaches to bank management in advocating not simply the avoidance of risk but the optimization of it—a strategy that is accomplished by mixing and matching various risky assets, including investment instruments traditionally shunned by bankers, such as forward and futures contracts, options, and other so-called "derivatives" (securities whose value derives from that of other, underlying assets). Despite the level of risk associated with them, derivatives can be used to hedge losses on other risky assets. For example, a bank manager may wish to protect his bank against a possible fall in the value of its bond holdings if interest rates rise during the following three months. In this case he can purchase a three-month forward contract— that is, by selling the bonds for delivery in three months' time—or, alternatively, take a short position—a promise to sell a particular amount at a specific price—in bond futures. If interest rates do happen to rise during that period, profits from the forward contract or short futures position should completely offset the loss in the capital value of the bonds. The goal is not to change

JPMorgan Chase CEO Jamie Dimon testifies before the Senate Banking, Housing and Urban Affairs Committee in 2012. Tom Williams/CQ Roll Call/Getty Images

MR. JAMES DIMON

the expected portfolio return but rather to reduce the variance of the return, thereby keeping the actual return closer to its expected value.

The risk management approach relies upon techniques, such as value at risk, or VAR (which measures the maximum likely loss on a portfolio during the next 100 days or so), that quantify overall risk exposure. One shortcoming of such risk measures is that they generally fail to consider high-impact, low-probability events, such as the bombing of the Central Bank of Sri Lanka in 1996 or the September 11 attacks in 2001. Another is that poorly selected or poorly monitored hedge investments can become significant liabilities in themselves, as occurred when the U.S. bank JPMorgan Chase lost more than $3 billion in trades of credit-based derivatives in 2012. For this reason, traditional bank-management tools, including reliance upon bank capital, must continue to play a role in risk management.

THE ROLE OF BANK CAPITAL

Because even the best risk management techniques cannot guarantee against losses, banks cannot rely on deposits alone to fund their investments. Funding also comes from share owners' equity, which means that bank managers must concern themselves with the value of the bank's equity capital as well as the composition of the bank's assets and liabilities. A bank's shareholders, however, are residual claimants, meaning that they may share in the bank's profits but are also the first to bear any losses stemming from bad loans or failed investments.

When the value of a bank's assets declines, shareholders bear the loss, at least up to the point at which their shares become worthless, while depositors stand to suffer only if losses mount high enough to exhaust the bank's equity, rendering the bank insolvent. In that case, the bank may be closed and its assets liquidated, with depositors (and, after them, if anything remains, other creditors) receiving prorated shares of the proceeds. Where bank deposits are not insured or otherwise guaranteed by government authorities, bank equity capital serves as depositors' principal source of security against bank losses. Deposit guarantees, whether explicit (as with deposit insurance) or implicit (as when government authorities are expected to bail out failing banks), can have the unintended consequence of reducing a bank's equity capital, for which such guarantees are a substitute. Regulators have in turn attempted to compensate for this effect by regulating bank capital. For example, the first (1988) and second (2004) Basel Accords (Basel I and Basel II), which were implemented within the European Union and, to a limited extent, in the United States, established minimum capital requirements for different banks based on formulas that attempted to account for the risks to which each is exposed. Thus, Basel I established an 8 percent capital-to-asset ratio target, with bank assets weighted according to the risk of loss; weights ranged from zero (for top-rated government securities) to one (for some corporate bonds). Following the global financial crisis of 2008–09, a new agreement, known as Basel III (2010), increased capital requirements and imposed other safeguards in rules that would be implemented gradually through early 2019.

CHAPTER FOUR

REGULATION OF COMMERCIAL BANKS

For most developed countries the late 20th century was marked by a notable easing of regulations and restrictions in the banking industry. In the United States, for example, many regulations had originated in response to problems experienced during the Great Depression, especially in 1933, when the federal government closed the country's banks and permitted only those deemed solvent to reopen. By the end of the century the risk of widespread economic failure, such as that experienced in the Great Depression, was widely regarded as unlikely. That perception changed dramatically in 2008, however, when a steep decline in the value of mortgage-backed securities precipitated a global financial crisis and the worst economic downturn in the United States since the Great Depression. Legislation subsequently adopted in the United States partially restored some Depression-era regulations and imposed significant new restrictions on derivatives trading by banks.

ENTRY, BRANCHING, AND FINANCIAL-SERVICES RESTRICTIONS

Historically, many countries restricted entry into the banking business by granting special charters to select

President Franklin Delano Roosevelt signs the Glass-Steagall Act on June 16, 1933. © AP Images

firms. While the practice of granting charters has become obsolete, many countries effectively limit or prevent foreign banks or subsidiaries from entering their banking markets and thereby insulate their domestic banking industries from foreign competition.

In the United States through much of the 20th century, a combination of federal and state regulations, such as the Banking Act of 1933 (also known as the Glass-Steagall Act), prohibited interstate banking, prevented banks from trading in securities and insurance, and established the Federal Deposit Insurance Corporation (FDIC). Although the intent of the Depression-era legislation was the prevention of banking collapses, in many cases states prohibited statewide branch banking owing to the political influence of small-town bankers interested in limiting their competitors by creating geographic monopolies. Eventually competition from nonbank financial services firms, such as investment companies, loosened the banks' hold on their local markets. In large cities and small towns alike, securities firms and insurance companies began marketing a range of liquid financial instruments, some of which could serve as checking accounts. Rapid changes in financial structure and the increasingly competitive supply of financial services led to the passage of the Depository Institutions Deregulation and Monetary Control Act in 1980. Its principal objectives were to improve monetary control and equalize its cost among depository institutions, to remove impediments to competition for funds by depository institutions while allowing the small saver a market rate of return, and to expand the availability of financial services to the public and reduce competitive inequalities between the financial institutions offering them. In 1994, interstate branch banking became legal in the United States through the passage of the Riegle-Neal Interstate Banking and Branching Efficiency Act. Finally, in 1999 the Financial Services Modernization Act, also known as the Gramm-Leach-Bliley Act, repealed provisions of the Glass-Steagall Act that had prevented banks, securities firms, and insurance companies from entering each other's markets, allowing for a series of mergers that created the country's first "megabanks."

INTEREST RATE CONTROLS

One of the oldest forms of bank regulation consists of laws restricting the rates of interest bankers are allowed to charge on loans or to pay on deposits. Ancient and medieval Christians held it to be immoral for a lender to earn interest from a venture that did not involve substantial risk of loss. However, this injunction was relatively easy to circumvent: interest could be excused if the lender could demonstrate that the loan was risky or that it entailed a sacrifice of some profitable investment opportunity. Interest also could be built into currency-exchange charges, with money lent in one currency and repaid (at an artificially enhanced exchange rate) in another. Finally, the taint of usury could be removed by recasting loans as investment-share sale and repurchase agreements—not unlike contemporary overnight repurchase agreements. Over time, as church doctrines were reinterpreted to accommodate the needs of business, such devices became irrelevant, and the term *usury* came to refer only to excessive interest charges. Islamic law also prohibits the collection of interest. Consequently, in most Muslim countries financial intermediation is based not on debt contracts involving explicit interest payments but on profit-and-loss-sharing arrangements, in which banks and their depositors assume a share of ownership of their creditors' enterprises. (This was the case in some medieval Christian arrangements as well.) Despite the complexity of the Islamic approach, especially with regard to contracts, effective banking systems developed as alternatives to their Western counterparts. Yet during the 1960s and early '70s, when nominal market rates of interest exceeded 20 percent in much of the world, Islamic-style banks risked being eclipsed by Western-style banks that could more readily adjust their lending terms to reflect changing market conditions. Oil revenues eventually improved the demand for Islamic banking, and by the early 21st century hundreds of Islamic-style financial institutions existed around the world, handling hundreds of billions of dollars in annual transactions. Consequently, some larger multinational banks in the West began to offer banking services consistent with Islamic law.

The strict regulation of lending rates—that is, the setting of maximum rates, or the outright prohibition of interest-taking—has been less common outside Muslim countries. Markets are far more effective than regulations at influencing interest rates, and the wide variety of loans, all of which involve differing degrees of risk, make the design and enforcement of such regulations difficult. By the 21st century most countries had stopped regulating the rate of interest paid on deposits.

MANDATORY CASH RESERVES

Minimum cash reserves have been a long-established form of bank regulation. The requirement that each bank maintain a minimum reserve of base money has been justified on the grounds that it reduces the bank's exposure to liquidity risk (insolvency) and aids the central bank's efforts to maintain control over national money stocks (by preserving a more stable relationship between the outstanding quantity of base money, which central banks are able directly to regulate, and the outstanding quantity of bank money).

A third objective of legal reserve requirements is that of securing government revenue. Binding reserve requirements contribute to the overall demand for basic money—which consists of central bank deposit credits and notes—and therefore enhance as well the demand for government securities that central banks typically hold as backing for their outstanding liabilities. A greater portion of available savings is thus channeled from commercial bank customers to the public sector. Bank depositors feel the effect of the transfer in the form of lowered net interest earnings on their deposits. The higher the minimum legal reserve ratio, the greater the proportion of savings transferred to the public sector.

Some economists have challenged the concept of legal reserve requirements by arguing that they are not necessary for effective monetary control. They also suggest that such requirements could be self-defeating; if the requirements are rigidly enforced, banks may resist drawing upon reserves altogether if doing so would mean violating the requirement.

CAPITAL STANDARDS

Bank capital protects bank depositors from losses by treating bank shareholders as "residual claimants" who risk losing their equity share if a bank is unable to honour its commitments to depositors. One means of ensuring an adequate capital cushion for banks has been the imposition of minimum capital standards in tandem with the establishment of required capital-to-asset ratios, which vary depending upon a bank's exposure to various risks. The most important step in this direction has been the implementation of the various Basel Accords.

NATIONALIZATION

Instead of attempting to regulate privately owned banks, governments sometimes prefer to run the banks

themselves. Both Karl Marx and Vladimir Lenin advocated the centralization of credit through the establishment of a single monopoly bank, and the nationalization of Russia's commercial banks was one of the first reform measures taken by the Bolsheviks when they came to power in 1917. Nonetheless, the Soviet Union found itself without a functioning monetary system following the Bolsheviks' reform.

Nationalized banks can be found in many partially socialized or mixed economies, especially in less-developed economies, where they sometimes coexist with privately owned banks. There they are justified on the grounds that nationalized banks are a necessary element of a developing country's economic growth. The general performance of such banks, like that of banks in socialist economies, has been poor, largely because of a lack of incentives needed to promote efficiency. Some have experienced higher delinquency rates on their loans, owing in part to government-mandated lending to insolvent enterprises.

Morgan Stanley CEO John Mack and Citigroup CEO Vikram Pandit leave a Treasury Department meeting on October 13, 2008, amid the government bailouts of the largest banks during the financial crisis. Mark Wilson/Getty Images

There are exceptions, however. While nationalized banks have tended to be overstaffed, slow in providing services to borrowers, and unprofitable, the State Bank of India is recognized for customer satisfaction, and many state-owned banks in South Asia perform on a par with their private-sector counterparts.

DEPOSIT INSURANCE

Most countries require banks to participate in a national insurance program, known as deposit insurance, intended to protect bank deposit holders from losses that could occur in the event of a bank failure.

RATIONALE FOR DEPOSIT INSURANCE

Although bank deposit insurance is primarily viewed as a means of protecting individual (and especially small) bank depositors, its more subtle purpose is one of protecting entire national banking and payments systems by preventing costly bank runs and panics. In a theoretical scenario, adverse news or rumours concerning an individual bank or small group of banks could prompt holders of uninsured deposits to withdraw all their holdings. This immediately affects the banks directly concerned, but large-scale withdrawals may prompt a run on other banks as well, especially when depositors lack information on the soundness of their own bank's investments. This can lead them to withdraw money from healthy banks merely through a suspicion that their banks might be as troubled as the ones that are failing. Bank runs can thereby spread by contagion and, in

PANIC

In economics, the term *panic* refers to a severe financial disturbance, such as widespread bank failures, feverish stock speculation followed by a market crash, or a climate of fear caused by economic crisis or anticipation of such a crisis. It is applied only to the initial, violent stage of financial upheaval rather than to the whole decline in the business cycle.

Until the 19th century, economic fluctuations were largely connected with shortages of goods, market expansion, and speculation (as in the South Sea Bubble). Panics in industrialized societies since the 19th century have reflected the increasing complexity of advanced economies. The Panic of 1857 in the U.S., for example, had its seeds in the railroads' defaulting on their bonds and in the decline in the value of railroad securities. Its effects were complex, including not only the closing of many banks but also severe unemployment in the U.S. and a money-market panic in Europe. The Panic of 1873, which began with financial crises in Vienna and New York, marked the start of a long-term contraction in the world economy. The most infamous panic began with the U.S. stock-market crash of 1929 and the start of the Great Depression.

the worst-case scenario, generate a banking panic, with depositors converting all of their deposits into cash. Furthermore, because the actual cash reserves held by any bank amount to only a fraction of its immediately withdrawable (e.g., "demand" or "sight") deposits, a generalized banking panic will ultimately result not only in massive depositor losses but also in the wholesale collapse of the banking system, with all the disruption of payments and credit flows any such collapse must entail.

HOW DEPOSIT INSURANCE WORKS

Deposit insurance eliminates or reduces depositors' incentive to stage bank runs. In the simplest scenario, where deposits (or deposits up to a certain value) are fully insured, all or most deposit holders enjoy full protection of their deposits, including any promised interest payments, even if their bank does fail. Banks that become insolvent for reasons unrelated to panic might be quietly sold to healthy banks, immediately closed and liquidated, or (temporarily) taken over by the insuring agency.

ORIGINS OF DEPOSIT INSURANCE

Although various U.S. state governments experimented with deposit insurance prior to the establishment of the FDIC in 1933, most of these experiments failed (in some cases because the banks engaged in excessive risk taking). The concept of national deposit insurance had garnered little support until large numbers of bank failures during the first years of the Great Depression revived public interest in banking reform. In an era of bank failures, voters increasingly favoured deposit insurance as an essential protection against losses. Strong opposition to nationwide branch banking (which would have eliminated small and underdiversified banks through a substantial consolidation of the banking industry), combined with opposition from unit banks (banks that lacked branch networks), prevailed against larger banks

A special session of Congress called by President Roosevelt on March 9, 1933, to introduce the Emergency Banking Relief Act amid the Great Depression. © AP Images

and the Roosevelt administration, which supported nationwide branch banking; this resulted in the inclusion of federal deposit insurance as a component of the Banking Act of 1933. Originally the law provided coverage for individual deposits up to $5,000. The limit was increased on several occasions since that time, reaching $250,000 for interest-bearing accounts in 2010.

Deposit insurance has become common in banking systems worldwide. The particulars of these schemes can differ substantially; some countries require coverage that amounts to only a few hundred U.S. dollars, while others offer blanket guarantees that cover nearly 100 percent of deposited moneys. In 1994 a uniform deposit-insurance scheme became a component of the European Union's single banking market.

Ironically, deposit insurance has the potential to undermine market discipline because it does nothing to discourage depositors from patronizing risky banks. Because depositors bear little or none of the risk associated with bank failures, they will often select banks that pay the highest non-risk-adjusted deposit rates of interest while ignoring safety considerations altogether. This can encourage bankers to attract more customers by paying higher rates of interest, but in so doing, the banks must direct their business toward loans and investments that carry higher potential returns but also greater risk. In extreme cases losses from risky investments may even bankrupt the deposit insurance program, causing deposit guarantees to be honoured only through resort to general tax revenues. This was, in essence, what happened in the United States savings and loan crisis of the 1980s, which bankrupted the FDIC.

Most countries insure bank deposits up to a certain amount, with few offering blanket deposit coverage (i.e., 100 percent of the amount any depositor holds with a bank). In the United States, blanket deposit coverage was established for non-interest-bearing transaction accounts (accounts that allow an unlimited number of withdrawals and transfers) by the Dodd-Frank Wall Street Reform and Consumer Protection Act (2010).

CHAPTER FIVE

CENTRAL BANKING

Central banks maintain accounts for, and extend credit to, commercial banks and, in most instances, their sponsoring governments, but they generally do not do business with the public at large. Because they have the right to issue fiat money, most central banks serve as their nations' (or, in the case of the European Central Bank, several nations') only source of paper currency. The resulting monopoly of paper currency endows central banks with significant market influence as well as

The official seal of the United States Federal Reserve. fliegenwulf/Shutterstock.com a certain revenue stream, which is known as seigniorage, after the lords or seigneurs of medieval France who enjoyed the privilege of minting their own coins.

Contemporary central banks manage a broad range of public responsibilities, the first and most familiar of which is the prevention of banking crises. This responsibility involves supplying additional cash reserves to commercial banks that risk failure due to extraordinary reserve losses. Other responsibilities include managing the growth of national money stocks (and, indirectly, fostering economic stability by preventing wide fluctuations in general price levels, interest rates, and exchange rates), regulating commercial banks, and serving as the sponsoring government's fiscal agent—e.g., by purchasing government securities.

ORIGINS OF CENTRAL BANKING

The concept of central banking can be traced to medieval public banks. In Barcelona the Taula de Canvi (Municipal Bank of Deposit) was established in 1401 for the safekeeping of city and private deposits, but it was also expected to help fund Barcelona's government (particularly the financing of military expenses), which it did by receiving tax payments and issuing bonds—first for Barcelona's municipal government and later for the larger Catalan government. The Taula was not permitted to lend to any other entity. During the 1460s, however, excessive demands for lending caused the Taula to suspend the convertibility of its deposits, and this led to its liquidation and reorganization.

The success of later public banks generally depended upon the extent to which their sponsoring governments valued long-term bank safety over loan flexibility. During the 17th and 18th centuries the Amsterdamsche Wisselbank was an especially successful example. The bank's conservative lending policy allowed it to maintain reserves that fully covered its outstanding notes and thereby rendered it invulnerable even to the major panic provoked by Louis XIV's unexpected invasion of the Netherlands in 1672. Although the Wisselbank had not been required to maintain 100 percent backing for its notes prior to 1802, its reserves shrank and its reputation suffered after it granted large-scale loans to the Dutch East India Company and the Dutch government.

The Bank of England, founded in 1694 for the purpose of advancing £1.2 million to the British government to fund its war against France, eventually became the world's most powerful and influential financial institution. It was the first public bank to assume most of the characteristics of modern central banks, including acceptance, by the late 19th century, of an official role in preserving the integrity of England's banking and monetary system (as opposed to merely looking after its own profits). By 1800 the Bank of England had become the country's only limited-liability joint-stock bank, its charter having denied other banks the right to issue banknotes (then an essential source of bank funding). Its size and prestige encouraged deposits from other banks and thereby streamlined the process of interbank debt settlement and confirmed the Bank of England's status as the "bankers' bank."

There were cracks, however, in the Bank of England's near-monopoly power. Although private banknotes had ceased to circulate in London by 1780, they survived in the provinces, where the Bank of England was prohibited from establishing branches. Following the Panic of 1825—a sharp economic downturn associated with a steep decline in commodities prices—dozens of county banks risked insolvency and failure. The government responded by rescinding the prohibition on joint-stock banking, though only for banks located at least 65 miles (105 km) from the centre of London. The same reform also allowed the Bank of England to set up provincial branches, but this last measure did not prevent the establishment of almost 100 joint-stock banks of issue between 1826 and 1836. The Bank of England's monopoly was thus partially infringed. Two further measures, however, ultimately served to enhance its power, causing other banks to rely upon it as a source of currency for their routine needs as well as during emergencies. An 1833 act made Bank of England notes legal tender for sums above £5, which strengthened the tendency for the nation's metallic reserves to concentrate in one place. And Peel's Act of 1844 (formally known as the Bank Charter Act) in turn awarded the Bank of England an eventual monopoly of paper currency by fixing the maximum note issues of other banks at levels outstanding just prior to the act's passage while requiring banks to give up their note-issuing privileges upon merging with or being absorbed by other banks.

In England the passage of Peel's Act marked a practical victory for proponents of currency monopoly over those who favoured "free banking"—that is, a system in which all banks were equally free to issue redeemable paper notes. The free bankers maintained that Peel's Act allowed the Bank of England to exercise an unhealthy influence upon the banking system and deprived other banks of the strength and flexibility they needed to tide themselves through financial crises. Proponents of currency monopoly, on the other hand, favoured having one bank alone bear ultimate responsibility both for preserving the long-term integrity of the currency and for preventing—or at least containing—financial crises. Although he himself favoured free banking, Walter Bagehot, then editor of *The Economist* magazine, played a key role in shaping the modern view of central banks as essential lenders of last resort. In the book *Lombard Street* (1873), he outlined the critical responsibilities of monopoly banks of issue (such as the Bank of England) during episodes of financial crises, and he emphasized the need for such banks to put the interests of the economy as a whole ahead of their own interests by keeping open lines of credit to other solvent but temporarily illiquid banks. These concepts of central banking led to the establishment of similar institutions in France, Germany, and elsewhere.

MODERN DEVELOPMENTS

In the United States, state banking laws prohibiting branch banking, and Civil War-era restrictions on note issuance, rendered the banking system vulnerable to periodic crises. The crises eventually gave rise to a banking reform movement, the ultimate outcome of which was the passage of the Federal Reserve Act in 1913 and the establishment of the Federal Reserve System.

After 1914 central banking spread rapidly to other parts of the world, and by the outbreak of World War II most countries had adopted it. The exceptions were the European colonies, which tended to rely on alternative currency arrangements. When they achieved

A production line at the Douglas Aircraft factory during World War II. Popperfoto/Getty Images

independence after the war, however, most of them adopted central banking. After the 1970s several nations that had experienced recurring bouts of hyperinflation chose to abandon their central banking arrangements in favour of either modified currency-board-like systems or official "dollarization" (that is, the use of Federal Reserve dollars in lieu of their own distinct paper currency).

The worldwide spread of central banking during the 20th century coincided with the worldwide abandonment of metallic monetary systems, meaning that central banks effectively replaced gold and silver as the world's ultimate sources of base money. Central banks are therefore responsible for supplying most of the world's circulating paper currency, supplying commercial banks with cash reserves, and, indirectly, regulating the quantity of commercial bank deposits and loans.

INFLUENCE OF CENTRAL BANKS

The chief feature that distinguishes central banks from commercial banks is their ability to issue fiat paper notes, which in most countries are the only available form of paper currency and the only form of money having unlimited legal-tender status. Besides being held by the general public, central banknotes also serve, together with central bank deposit credits, as the cash reserves of commercial banks. It is the central banks' monopoly of paper currency and bank reserves that allows them to exercise control over the total supply of money (including commercial bank deposits) available in the economies over which their monopoly privileges extend. By altering national money stocks, central banks indirectly influence rates of spending and inflation and, to a far more limited extent, rates of employment and the production of goods and services. Central banks also can influence the fate of individual banks, and indeed the stability of the banking industry as a whole, by granting or refusing emergency assistance in their role as lender of last resort. Finally, central banks typically take part in the regulation of commercial banks. In this capacity they may enforce a variety of rules governing such things as cash reserve ratios, interest rates, investment portfolios, equity capital, and entry into the banking industry.

MONETARY CONTROL

Central banks can control national money stocks in two ways: directly, by limiting their issues of paper currency, and indirectly, by altering available supplies of bank reserves and thereby influencing the value of the deposit credits that banks are capable of maintaining. Generally speaking, however, control is secured entirely through the market for bank reserves, with currency supplied to banks on demand in exchange for existing reserve credits.

OPEN-MARKET OPERATIONS

In most industrialized countries the supply of bank reserves is mainly regulated by means of central bank sales and purchases of government securities, foreign exchange, and other assets in secondary or open asset markets. When a central bank purchases assets in the open market, it pays for them with a check drawn upon itself. The seller then deposits the check with a commercial bank, which sends the check to the central bank for settlement in the form of a credit to the bank's reserve account. Banking system reserves are thus increased by the value of the open-market purchase. Open-market asset sales have the opposite consequence, with the value of checks written by securities dealers being deducted from the reserve accounts of the dealers' banks. The principal merit of open-market operations as an instrument of monetary control is that such operations allow central banks to exercise full control over outstanding stocks of basic money.

MONEY SUPPLY

The money supply consists of the liquid assets held by individuals and banks. It includes coin, currency, and demand deposits (checking accounts). Some economists consider time and savings deposits to be part of the money supply because such deposits can be managed by governmental action and are involved in aggregate economic activity. These deposits are nearly as liquid as currency and demand deposits. Other economists believe that deposits in mutual savings banks, savings and loan associations, and credit unions should be counted as part of the money supply.

The Federal Reserve Board in the United States and the Bank of England in the United Kingdom regulate the money supply to stabilize their respective economies. The Federal Reserve Board, for example, can buy or sell government securities, thereby expanding or contracting the money supply.

MINIMUM RESERVE REQUIREMENTS

Two other instruments of monetary control of considerable importance are changes in mandated bank reserve requirements (minimum legal ratios of bank cash reserves to deposits of various kinds) and changes in the discount rate (the interest rate a central bank charges on loans made to commercial banks and other financial intermediaries). Changes in reserve requirements work not by altering the total outstanding value of bank reserves but by altering the total value of deposits supported by available cash reserves.

THE DISCOUNT RATE

The role of discount-rate changes is frequently misunderstood by the general public. Instead of purchasing assets on the open market, a central bank can purchase assets directly from a commercial bank. Traditionally such direct purchasing was known as "discounting" because assets were acquired at a discount from their face or maturity value, with the discount rate embodying an implicit rate of interest. Today central bank support to commercial banks often takes the form of outright loans, even in systems (such as that of the United States) in which official central bank lending rates continue to be referred to as "discount" rates.

Confusion arises because it is often the case that, in setting their own discount rates, central banks are able to influence market lending rates. In practice, most central banks supply relatively little base money through their discount windows, often restricting their discount or lending operations mainly to troubled banks but even denying funds to some of those. Consequently, there may be no connection at all between the rates central banks charge commercial banks and other (including commercial-bank) lending rates. Some central banks have contributed to misunderstandings by using changes in their discount rates as a means of signaling their intention either to increase or to reduce the availability of bank reserves, with the actual easing or tightening of bank reserve market conditions being accomplished, more often than not, by means of open-market operations.

INFLATION TARGETS

Although most central banks (at least those not bound by a fixed exchange-rate commitment) continue to pursue a variety of objectives, economists generally believe that their principal aim should be long-term price stability, meaning an annual rate of general price inflation that is within the range of 0 to 3 percent. While other popular monetary policy objectives, including the financing of government expenditures, combating unemployment, and "smoothing" or otherwise regulating interest rates, are not necessarily at loggerheads with this goal, failure to subordinate such objectives to that of price-level stability has often proved to be a recipe for high inflation.

INFLUENCE ON MARKET RATES OF INTEREST

It is sometimes assumed that, by setting their own discount rates, central banks are able to influence, if not completely control, general market lending rates. In truth, most central banks supply relatively little base money in the form of direct loans or discounts to commercial banks. Central banks wield the greatest influence on rates that banks charge each other for short-term, especially overnight, funds. In some countries overnight interbank lending rates (such as the Federal Funds Rate in the United States, the London Interbank Offered Rate, or LIBOR, in England, and the Tokyo Interbank Offered Rate, or TIBOR, in Japan) function as important indirect guides to the central bank's monetary policy. Yet even in this respect the ability of central banks to influence inflation-adjusted interest rates is very limited, especially in the long term.

"LAST RESORT" LENDING

In its role as a lender of last resort, a central bank offers financial support to individual banking firms. Central banks perform this role to prevent such banks from failing prematurely and, more important, to prevent a general loss of confidence that could trigger widespread runs on a country's banks.

Such a banking panic can involve large-scale withdrawals of currency from the banking system, which, by exhausting bank reserves, might cause the banking system to collapse, depriving firms of access to an essential source of funding while making it extremely difficult for the central bank to steer clear of a deflationary crisis. By standing ready to provide aid to troubled banks and thereby assuring depositors that at least some of the economy's banking firms are in no danger of failing, central banks make the challenge of monetary control easier while maintaining the flow of bank credit.

MAJOR CENTRAL BANKS

Among the most important central banks in the world are the Federal Reserve of the United States, the Bank of England, and the Banque de France (Bank of France).

FEDERAL RESERVE SYSTEM

The Federal Reserve System is the central banking authority of the United States. It acts as a fiscal agent for

Left to right, Janet Yellen, Peter Diamond, and Sarah Bloom Raskin, nominees for the Federal Reserve Board of Governors, are sworn in during a hearing of the Senate Committee on Banking, Housing, and Urban Affairs on July 15, 2010. Bloomberg/Getty Images

the U.S. government, is custodian of the reserve accounts of commercial banks, makes loans to commercial banks, and oversees the supply of currency, including coin, in coordination with the U.S. Mint. The system was created by the Federal Reserve Act, which President Woodrow Wilson signed into law on December 23, 1913. It consists of the Board of Governors of the Federal Reserve System, the 12 Federal Reserve banks, the Federal Open Market Committee, and the Consumer Financial Protection Bureau (CFPB), which was authorized in 2010 by the Dodd-Frank Act (the CFPB assumed some functions of the former Consumer Advisory Council, which existed from 1976 to 2011). There are several thousand member banks.

The seven-member Board of Governors of the Federal Reserve System determines the reserve requirements of the member banks within statutory limits, reviews and determines the discount rates established by the 12 Federal Reserve banks, and reviews the budgets of the reserve banks. The Chairman of the Board of Governors is appointed to a four-year term by the president of the United States.

A Federal Reserve bank is a privately owned corporation established pursuant to the Federal Reserve Act to serve the public interest. It is governed by a board of nine directors, six of whom are elected by the member banks and three of whom are appointed by the Board of Governors of the Federal Reserve System. The 12 Federal Reserve banks are located in Boston; New York City; Philadelphia; Chicago; San Francisco; Cleveland, Ohio; Richmond, Virginia; Atlanta, Georgia; St. Louis, Missouri; Minneapolis, Minnesota; Kansas City, Missouri; and Dallas, Texas.

The 12-member Federal Open Market Committee, consisting of the seven members of the Board of Governors, the president of the Federal Reserve Bank of New York, and four members elected by the Federal Reserve banks, is responsible for the determination of Federal Reserve bank policy to encourage long-term objectives of price stability (i.e., controlling inflation through the adjustment of interest rates) and economic growth.

The Federal Reserve System exercises its regulatory powers in several ways, the most important of which may be classified as instruments of direct or indirect control. One form of direct control can be exercised by adjusting the legal reserve ratio—i.e., the proportion of its deposits that a member bank must hold in its reserve account—thus increasing or reducing the amount of new loans that the commercial banks can make. Because loans give rise to new deposits, the potential money supply is, in this way, expanded or reduced.

The money supply may also be influenced through manipulation of the discount rate, which is the rate of interest charged by Federal Reserve banks on short-term secured loans to member banks. Since these loans are typically sought by banks to maintain reserves at their required level, an increase in the cost of such loans has an effect similar to that of increasing the reserve requirement.

The classic method of indirect control is through open-market operations, first widely used in the 1920s and now employed daily to make small adjustments in the market. Federal Reserve bank sales or purchases of securities on the open market tend to reduce or increase the size of commercial-bank reserves—e.g., when the Federal Reserve sells securities, the purchasers pay for them with checks drawn on their deposits, thereby reducing the reserves of the banks on which the checks are drawn.

The three instruments of control described here have been conceded to be more effective in preventing inflation in times of high economic activity than in bringing about revival from a period of depression. A supplemental control occasionally used by the Federal Reserve Board is that of changing the margin requirements involved in the purchase of securities.

The Federal Reserve has broad supervisory and regulatory authority over state-chartered banks and bank holding companies, as well as foreign banks operating in the United States. It is also involved in maintaining the credit rights of consumers. One of the longest chairmanships of the Federal Reserve Board was held by Alan

Greenspan, who took office in August 1987 and held the post until January 2006.

BANK OF ENGLAND

The Bank of England is the central bank of the United Kingdom. Its headquarters are in the central financial district of the City of London.

The Bank of England was incorporated by act of Parliament in 1694 with the immediate purpose of raising funds to allow the English government to wage war against France in the Low Countries. A royal charter allowed the bank to operate as a joint-stock bank with limited liability. No other joint-stock banks were permitted in England and Wales until 1826. This special status and its position as the government's banker gave the bank considerable competitive advantages.

The bank was located first in Mercers' Hall and then in Grocers' Hall, but it was moved to its permanent location on Threadneedle Street in the 1730s. By that time it had become the largest and most prestigious financial institution in England, and its banknotes were widely circulated. As a result, it became banker to other banks, which, by maintaining balances with the Bank of England, could settle debts among themselves. The bank was threatened by the economic instability that accompanied the French Revolution and Napoleonic Wars, but its standing was also considerably enhanced by its actions in raising funds for Britain's involvement in those conflicts.

During the 19th century the bank gradually assumed the responsibilities of a central bank. In 1833 it began to print legal tender, and it undertook the roles of lender of last resort and guardian of the nation's gold reserves in the following few decades.

The bank was privately owned until 1946, when it was nationalized. It funds public borrowing, issues banknotes, and manages the country's gold and foreign-exchange reserves. It is an important adviser to the government on monetary policy and is largely responsible for implementing policy by its dealings in the money, bond, and foreign-exchange markets. The bank's freedom of action in this regard was considerably enhanced when it was given the power to determine short-term interest rates in 1997.

BANQUE DE FRANCE

The Banque de France (Bank of France), the national bank of France, was created in 1800 to restore confidence in the French banking system after the financial upheavals of the revolutionary period (1787–99). Headquarters are in Paris.

The bank listed among its founding shareholders Napoleon Bonaparte, members of his family, and several leading personalities of the time. Founded partly with state funds, but mainly with private capital, the bank was closely connected with the state from the beginning. The French government claimed a participation in the control of the bank through the appointment of the governor and two deputy governors, while the shareholders were represented by a board of 15 regents elected by the 200 largest shareholders.

The bank was initially granted the exclusive privilege to issue banknotes in Paris for a period of 15 years. It was later authorized to establish discount offices in towns where commercial requirements made this necessary, and it was subsequently empowered to exercise its privileges, including the privilege of note issue, in the towns where discount offices were established. Its note-issue privilege was extended to cover the whole of France in 1848 as a result of the transformation of nine provincial banks with note-issuing powers into branches of the bank. In 1946 the bank was nationalized, and its note-issue privilege was extended for an indefinite period.

Statutes approved in 1973 placed greater power with the bank's general council and gave the French minister of finance control over Banque de France's dividend payments and other uses of the bank's profits. The bank was privatized in 1993, a step taken partly in preparation for France's participation in the European Monetary System, whose member countries converted to a single currency, the euro, in 1999.

CHAPTER SIX

WORLD BANK

The World Bank (in full World Bank Group) is an international organization affiliated with the United Nations (UN) and designed to finance projects that enhance the economic development of member states. Headquartered in Washington, D.C., the bank is the largest source of financial assistance to developing countries. It also provides technical assistance and policy advice and supervises—on behalf of international creditors—the implementation of free-market reforms. Together with the International Monetary Fund (IMF) and the World Trade Organization, it plays a central role in overseeing economic policy and reforming public institutions in developing countries and defining the global macroeconomic agenda.

ORIGINS

Founded in 1944 at the UN Monetary and Financial Conference (commonly known as the Bretton Woods Conference), which was convened to establish a new, post-World War II international economic system, the World Bank officially began operations in June 1946. Its first loans were designed to aid the postwar reconstruction of western Europe. Beginning in the mid-1950s, it played a major role in financing investments in infrastructural projects in developing countries, including

Dr. Jim Yong Kim, president of the World Bank Group.
© AP Images

roads, hydroelectric dams, water and sewage facilities, maritime ports, and airports.

The World Bank Group comprises five constituent institutions: the International Bank for Reconstruction and Development (IBRD), the International Development Association (IDA), the International Finance Corporation (IFC), the Multilateral Investment Guarantee Agency (MIGA), and the International Centre for Settlement of Investment Disputes (ICSID). The IBRD provides loans at market rates of interest to middle-income developing countries and creditworthy lower-income countries. The IDA, founded in 1960, provides interest-free long-term loans, technical assistance, and policy advice to low-income developing countries in areas such as health, education, and rural development. Whereas the IBRD raises most of its funds on the world's capital markets, the IDA's lending operations are financed through contributions from developed countries. The IFC, operating in partnership with private investors, provides loans and loan guarantees and equity financing to business undertakings in developing countries. Loan guarantees and insurance to foreign investors against loss caused by noncommercial risks in developing countries are provided by the MIGA. Finally, the ICSID, which operates independently of the IBRD, is responsible for the settlement by conciliation or arbitration of investment disputes between foreign investors and their host developing countries.

From 1968 to 1981 the president of the World Bank was former U.S. secretary of defense Robert McNamara. Under his leadership the bank formulated the concept of "sustainable development," which attempted to reconcile economic growth and environmental protection

ROBERT MCNAMARA

(b. June 9, 1916, San Francisco, California, U.S.—
d. July 6, 2009, Washington, D.C.)

As U.S. secretary of defense from 1961 to 1968, Robert McNamara revamped Pentagon operations and played a major role in the country's military involvement in Vietnam.

After graduating from the University of California, Berkeley, in 1937, McNamara earned a graduate degree at the Harvard Business School (1939) and later joined the Harvard faculty. Disqualified from combat duty during World War II by poor vision, he developed logistical systems for bomber raids and statistical systems for monitoring troops and supplies.

After the war, McNamara was one of the "Whiz Kids" hired to revitalize the Ford Motor Company. His plans, including the institution of strict cost-accounting methods and the development of both compact and luxury models, met with success, and McNamara rose rapidly in the corporate ranks. In 1960 he became the first person outside the Ford family to assume presidency of the company.

Robert S. McNamara, 1967. Yoichi R. Okamoto, the Lyndon Baines Johnson Library and Museum/National Archives and Records Administration

(From left to right) *Gen. Earle G. Wheeler, Robert S. McNamara, Cyrus Vance, and Lt. Gen. David A. Burchinal at the Pentagon, Arlington, Virginia, 1964.* PHC Harold Wise, USN/U.S. Department of Defense

After just one month as Ford's president, however, McNamara resigned to join the Kennedy administration as secretary of defense. In his new post he successfully gained control of Pentagon operations and the military bureaucracy, encouraged the modernization of the armed forces, restructured budget procedures, and cut costs by refusing to spend money on what he believed were unnecessary or obsolete weapons systems. McNamara was also at the centre of a drive to alter U.S. military strategy from the "massive retaliation" of the Eisenhower years to a "flexIble response," emphasizing counterinsurgency techniques and second-strike nuclear-missile capability.

McNamara initially advocated deepening U.S. military involvement in Vietnam. On visits to South Vietnam

Robert S. McNamara, c. 1967. The Lyndon Baines Johnson Library and Museum

in 1962, 1964, and 1966, he publicly expressed optimism that the National Liberation Front and its North Vietnamese allies would soon abandon their attempt to overthrow the U.S.-backed Saigon regime. He became the government's chief spokesman for the day-to-day operations of the war and acted as President Lyndon B. Johnson's principal deputy in the war's prosecution.

As early as 1965, however, McNamara had privately begun to question the wisdom of U.S. military involvement in Vietnam, and by 1967 he was openly seeking a way to launch peace negotiations. He initiated a top-secret full-scale investigation of the American commitment to Vietnam (later published as *The Pentagon Papers*), came out in opposition to continued bombing of North Vietnam (for which he lost influence in the Johnson administration), and in February 1968 left the Pentagon to become president of the World Bank.

In his 13-year tenure as head of that institution, McNamara displayed what was generally regarded as great sensitivity to the needs of developing countries. He retired from the World Bank in 1981 but remained active in many other organizations. He addressed issues such as world hunger, East-West relations, and other policy matters. His policy papers were published in two volumes, and his book *Blundering into Disaster: Surviving the First Century in a Nuclear Age* (1986) discusses nuclear war.

In 1995 McNamara published a memoir, *In Retrospect: The Tragedy and Lessons of Vietnam*, in which he describes the anticommunist political climate of the era, mistaken assumptions of foreign policy, and misjudgments on the part of the military that combined to create the Vietnam debacle. In Errol Morris's documentary film *The Fog of War* (2003), McNamara discusses his career in the Pentagon as well as U.S. failures in Vietnam.

in developing countries. Another feature of the concept was its use of capital flows (in the form of development assistance and foreign investment) to developing countries as a means of narrowing the income gap between rich and poor countries. The bank has expanded its lending activities and, with its numerous research and policy divisions, has developed into a powerful and authoritative intergovernmental body.

ORGANIZATION

The World Bank is related to the UN, though it is not accountable either to the General Assembly or to the Security Council. Each of the bank's more than 180 member states are represented on the board of governors, which meets once a year. The governors are usually their countries' finance ministers or central bank governors. Although the board of governors has some influence on IBRD policies, actual decision-making power is wielded largely by the bank's 25 executive directors. Five major countries—the United States, Japan, Germany, the United Kingdom, and France—appoint their own executive directors. The other countries are grouped into regions, each of which elects one executive director. Throughout the World Bank's history, the bank president, who serves as chairman of the Executive Board, has been an American citizen.

Voting power is based on a country's capital subscription, which is based in turn on its economic resources. The wealthier and more developed countries constitute the bank's major shareholders and thus exercise greater power and influence. For example, at the beginning of the 21st century the United States exercised about one-sixth of the votes, more than double that of Japan, the second largest contributor. Because developing countries hold only a small number of votes, the system does not provide a significant voice for these countries, which are the primary recipients of World Bank loans and policy advice.

The bank obtains its funds from the capital subscriptions of member countries, bond flotations on the world's capital markets, and net earnings accrued from interest payments on IBRD and IFC loans. Approximately one-tenth of the subscribed capital is paid directly to the bank, with the remainder subject to call if required to meet obligations.

The World Bank is staffed by more than 9,000 people, roughly one-fourth of whom are posted in developing countries. The bank has more than 100 offices in member countries, and in many countries staff members serve directly as policy advisers to the ministry of finance and other ministries. The bank has consultative as well as informal ties with the world's financial markets and institutions and maintains links with nongovernmental organizations in both developed and developing countries.

DEBT AND POLICY REFORM

The debt crisis of the early 1980s—during which many developing countries were unable to service their external debt to multilateral lending institutions because of a slowdown in the world economy, high interest rates, a decline in commodity prices, and wide fluctuations in oil prices, among other factors—played a crucial role in the evolution of World Bank operations. The bank had become increasingly involved in shaping economic and social policies in indebted developing countries. As a condition of receiving loans, borrowing countries were required to implement stringent "structural adjustment programs," which typically included severe cuts in spending for health and education, the elimination of price controls, the liberalization of trade, the deregulation of the financial sector, and the privatization of state-run enterprises. Although intended to restore economic stability, these programs, which were applied in a large number of countries throughout the developing world, frequently resulted in increased levels of poverty, mounting unemployment, and a spiraling external debt. In the wake of the debt crisis, the World Bank focused its efforts on providing financial assistance in the form of balance-of-payments support and loans for infrastructural projects such as roads, port facilities, schools, and hospitals. Although emphasizing poverty alleviation and debt relief for the world's least developed countries, the bank has retained its commitment to economic stabilization policies that require the implementation of austerity measures by recipient countries.

The World Bank and the IMF played central roles in overseeing free-market reforms in eastern and central Europe after the fall of communism there in the 1980s and '90s. The reforms, which included the creation of bankruptcy and privatization programs, were controversial because they frequently led to the closure of state-run industrial enterprises. "Exit mechanisms" to allow for the liquidation of so-called "problem enterprises" were put into place, and labour laws were modified to enable enterprises to lay off unneeded workers. The larger state enterprises often were sold to foreign investors or divided into smaller, privately owned companies. In Hungary, for example, some 17,000 businesses were liquidated and 5,000 reorganized in 1992–93, leading to a substantial increase in unemployment. The World Bank also provided reconstruction loans to countries that suffered internal conflicts or other crises (e.g., the successor republics of former Yugoslavia in the late 1990s). This financial assistance did not succeed in rehabilitating productive infrastructure, however. In several countries the macroeconomic reforms resulted in increased inflation and a marked decline in the standard of living. In 2001 the World Bank announced its commitment to implementing the UN Millennium Development Goals, which had been adopted at a special session of the General Assembly in 2000 with the aim of significantly reducing poverty, hunger, and disease in developing countries by 2015. In response to the global financial crisis of 2008–09, the bank established new lending facilities designed to extend immediate assistance to vulnerable populations in affected developing countries and to preserve ongoing infrastructure projects.

The World Bank is the world's largest multilateral creditor institution, and as such many of the world's poorest countries owe it large sums of money. Indeed, for dozens of the most heavily indebted poor countries, the largest part of their external debt—in some cases constituting more than 50 percent—is owed to the World Bank and the multilateral regional development banks. According to some analysts, the burden of these debts—which according to the bank's statutes cannot be canceled or rescheduled—has perpetuated economic stagnation throughout the developing world.

CHAPTER SEVEN

BUSINESS FINANCE: THE SHORT TERM

The term *business finance* refers to the raising and managing of funds by business organizations. Planning, analysis, and control operations are responsibilities of the financial manager, who is usually close to the top of the organizational structure of a firm. In very large firms, major financial decisions are often made by a finance committee. In small firms, the owner-manager usually conducts the financial operations. Much of the day-to-day work of business finance is conducted by lower-level staff; their work includes handling cash receipts and disbursements, borrowing from commercial banks on a regular and continuing basis, and formulating cash budgets.

Financial decisions affect both the profitability and the risk of a firm's operations. An increase in cash holdings, for instance, reduces risk; but, because cash is not an earning asset, converting other types of assets to cash reduces the firm's profitability. Similarly, the use of additional debt can raise the profitability of a firm (because it is expanding its business with borrowed money), but more debt means more risk. Striking a balance—between risk and profitability—that will maintain the long-term value of a firm's securities is the task of finance.

FINANCIAL PLANNING AND CONTROL

Short-term financial operations are closely involved with the financial planning and control activities of a firm. These include financial ratio analysis, profit planning, financial forecasting, and budgeting.

FINANCIAL RATIO ANALYSIS

A firm's balance sheet contains many items that, taken by themselves, have no clear meaning. Financial ratio analysis is a way of appraising their relative importance.

An example of a company balance sheet. Daniel Padavona/ Shutterstock.com

The ratio of current assets to current liabilities, for example, gives the analyst an idea of the extent to which the firm can meet its current obligations. This is known as a liquidity ratio. Financial leverage ratios (such as the debt–asset ratio and debt as a percentage of total capitalization) are used to make judgments about the advantages to be gained from raising funds by the issuance of bonds (debt) rather than stock. Activity ratios, relating to the turnover of such asset categories as inventories, accounts receivable, and fixed assets, show how intensively a firm is employing its assets. A firm's primary operating objective is to earn a good return on its invested capital, and various profit ratios (profits as a percentage of sales, of assets, or of net worth) show how successfully it is meeting this objective.

Ratio analysis is used to compare a firm's performance with that of other firms in the same industry or with the performance of industry in general. It is also used to study trends in the firm's performance over time and thus to anticipate problems before they develop.

PROFIT PLANNING

Ratio analysis applies to a firm's current operating posture. But a firm must also plan for future growth. This requires decisions as to the expansion of existing operations and, in manufacturing, to the development of new product lines. A firm must choose between productive processes requiring various degrees of mechanization or automation—that is, various amounts of fixed capital in the form of machinery and equipment. This will increase fixed costs (costs that are relatively constant and do not decrease when the firm is operating at levels below full capacity). The higher the proportion of fixed costs to total costs, the higher must be the level of operation before profits begin, and the more sensitive profits will be to changes in the level of operation.

FINANCIAL FORECASTING

The financial manager must also make overall forecasts of future capital requirements to ensure that funds will be available to finance new investment programs. The first step in making such a forecast is to obtain an estimate of sales during each year of the planning period. This estimate is worked out jointly by the marketing, production, and finance departments. The marketing manager estimates demand; the production manager estimates capacity; and the financial manager estimates availability of funds to finance new accounts receivable, inventories, and fixed assets.

For the predicted level of sales, the financial manager estimates the funds that will be available from the company's operations and compares this amount with what will be needed to pay for the new fixed assets (machinery, equipment, etc.). If the growth rate exceeds 10 percent a year, asset requirements are likely to exceed internal sources of funds, so plans must be made to finance them by issuing securities. If, on the other hand, growth is slow, more funds will be generated than are required to support the estimated growth in sales. In this case, the financial manager will consider a number of alternatives, including increasing dividends to stockholders, retiring debt, using excess funds to acquire other firms, or, perhaps, increasing expenditures on research and development.

BUDGETING

Once a firm's general goals for the planning period have been established, the next step is to set up a detailed plan of operation—the budget. A complete budget system encompasses all aspects of the firm's operations over the planning period. It may even allow for changes in plans as required by factors outside the firm's control.

Budgeting is a part of the total planning activity of the firm, so it must begin with a statement of the firm's long-range plan. This plan includes a long-range sales forecast, which requires a determination of the number and types of products to be manufactured in the years encompassed by the long-range plan. Short-term budgets are formulated within the framework of the long-range plan. Normally, there is a budget for every individual product and for every significant activity of the firm.

Establishing budgetary controls requires a realistic understanding of the firm's activities. For example, a small firm purchases more parts and uses more labour and less machinery; a larger firm will buy raw materials and use machinery to manufacture end items. In consequence, the smaller firm should budget higher parts and labour cost ratios, while the larger firm should budget higher overhead cost ratios and larger investments in fixed assets. If standards are unrealistically high, frustrations and resentment will develop. If standards are unduly lax, costs will be out of control, profits will suffer, and employee morale will drop.

THE CASH BUDGET

One of the principal methods of forecasting the financial needs of a business is the cash budget, which predicts the combined effects of planned operations on the firm's cash flow. A positive net cash flow means that the firm will have surplus funds to invest. But if the cash budget indicates that an increase in the volume of operations will lead to a negative cash flow, additional financing will be required. The cash budget thus indicates the amount of funds that will be needed or available month by month or even week by week.

A firm may have excess cash for a number of reasons. There are likely to be seasonal or cyclic fluctuations in business. Resources may be deliberately accumulated as a protection against a number of contingencies. Since it is wasteful to allow large amounts of cash to remain idle, the financial manager will try to find short-term investments for sums that will be needed later. Short-term government or business securities can be selected and balanced in such a way that the financial manager obtains the maturities and risks appropriate to a firm's financial situation.

ACCOUNTS RECEIVABLE

Accounts receivable are the credit a firm gives its customers. The volume and terms of such credit vary among businesses and among countries; for manufacturing firms in the United States, for example, the ratio of receivables to sales ranges between 8 and 12 percent, representing an average collection period of approximately one month. The basis of a firm's credit policy

CREDIT BUREAU

A credit bureau is an organization that provides information to merchants or other businesses relating to the creditworthiness of current and prospective customers. Credit bureaus may be private enterprises or cooperatives operated by merchants in a particular locality. Users, such as credit card issuers or mortgage lenders, pay a membership charge or a fee based on the amount of service.

Cooperative credit bureaus, organized for the exchange of credit information among merchants, were known in some countries as early as 1860; most of their growth, however, occurred after World War I. Until then the small amount of credit granted was usually based on the merchant's personal knowledge of the customer. The primary function of many of the very early credit bureaus was to maintain a list of customers who were considered poor risks. As the use of consumer credit grew and populations became more mobile, businesses turned to credit bureaus for information regarding decisions on whether to grant credit.

At the turn of the 21st century, the leading credit bureaus in the United States (and in many European, Latin American, and Asian countries) were Equifax, Experian, and TransUnion. Their sources of information included the merchants or other businesses that had granted a customer credit in the past, employment records, landlords, public records, newspapers, and direct investigation. Any individual who has applied for a credit or charge account, a personal loan, insurance, or a job most likely has a credit record on file at one or more of these credit bureaus. The credit record, which is built and amended over time, contains information about one's income, debts, and credit payment history, as well as whether one has been sued, has been arrested, or has filed for bankruptcy. This information leads to the establishment of a credit score, a numerical representation of an individual's creditworthiness.

The development of e-commerce facilitated the accumulation and distribution of information on a nationwide and worldwide basis. The threat to privacy resulting from these practices was not immediately recognized. Independent agencies evaluate and compare the major credit bureaus, sometimes revealing errors and problems that have included mistaken identities, misapplied charges or debts, uncorrected errors, misleading information, and credit inconsistencies.

is the practice in its industry: generally, a firm must meet the terms offered by competitors. Much depends, of course, on the individual customer's credit standing.

To evaluate a customer as a credit risk, the credit manager considers what may be called the five Cs of credit: character, capacity, capital, collateral, and conditions. Information on these items is obtained from the firm's previous experience with the customer, supplemented by information from various credit associations and credit-reporting agencies. In reviewing a credit program, the financial manager should regard losses from bad debts as part of the cost of doing business. Accounts receivable represent an investment in the expansion of sales. The return on this investment can be calculated as in any capital budgeting problem.

INVENTORIES

Every company must carry stocks of goods and materials in inventory. The size of the investment in inventory depends on various factors, including the level of sales,

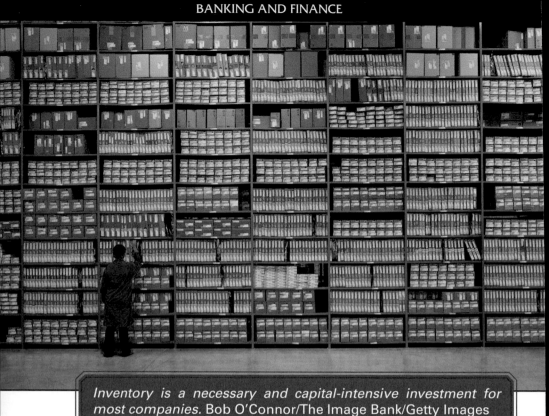

Inventory is a necessary and capital-intensive investment for most companies. Bob O'Connor/The Image Bank/Getty Images

the nature of the production processes, and the speed with which goods perish or become obsolete. The problems involved in managing inventories are basically the same as those in managing other assets, including cash. A basic stock must be on hand at all times. Because the unexpected may occur, it is also wise to have safety stocks, which represent the little extra needed to avoid the costs of not having enough. Additional amounts—anticipation stocks—may be required for meeting future growth needs. Finally, some inventory accumulation results from the economies of purchasing in large quantities. It is always cheaper to buy more than is immediately needed, whether of raw materials, money, or plant and equipment.

There is a standard procedure for determining the most economical amounts to order, one that relates purchasing requirements to costs and carrying charges (i.e., the cost of maintaining an inventory). While carrying charges rise as average inventory holdings increase, certain other costs (ordering costs and stock-out costs) fall as average inventory holdings rise. These two sets of costs constitute the total cost of ordering and carrying inventories, and it is fairly easy to calculate an optimal order size that will minimize total inventory costs. The advent of computerized inventory tracking fostered a practice known as just-in-time inventory management and thereby reduced the likelihood of excess or inadequate inventory stocks.

SHORT-TERM FINANCING

The main sources of short-term financing are (1) trade credit, (2) commercial bank loans, (3) commercial paper, a specific type of promissory note, and (4) secured loans.

TRADE CREDIT

A firm customarily buys its supplies and materials on credit from other firms, recording the debt as an account payable. This trade credit, as it is commonly called, is the largest single category of short-term credit. Credit terms are usually expressed with a discount for prompt payment. Thus, the seller may state that if payment is made within 10 days of the invoice date, a 2 percent cash discount will be allowed. If the cash discount is not taken, payment is due 30 days after the date of invoice. The cost of not taking cash discounts is the price of the credit.

COMMERCIAL BANK LOANS

Commercial bank lending appears on the balance sheet as notes payable and is second in importance to trade credit as a source of short-term financing. Banks occupy a pivotal position in the short-term and intermediate-term money markets. As a firm's financing needs grow, banks are called upon to provide additional funds. A single loan obtained from a bank by a business firm is not different in principle from a loan obtained by an individual. The firm signs a conventional promissory note. Repayment is made in a lump sum at maturity or in installments throughout the life of the loan. A line of credit, as distinguished from a single loan, is a formal or informal understanding between the bank and the borrower as to the maximum loan balance the bank will allow at any one time.

COMMERCIAL PAPER

Commercial paper, a third source of short-term credit, consists of well-established firms' promissory notes sold primarily to other businesses, insurance companies, pension funds, and banks. Commercial paper is issued for periods varying from two to six months. The rates on prime commercial paper vary, but they are generally slightly below the rates paid on prime business loans. A basic limitation of the commercial-paper market is that its resources are limited to the excess liquidity that corporations, the main suppliers of funds, may have at any particular time. Another disadvantage is the impersonality of the dealings: a bank is much more likely to help a good customer weather a storm than is a commercial-paper dealer.

SECURED LOANS

Most short-term business loans are unsecured, which means that an established company's credit rating qualifies it for a loan. It is ordinarily better to borrow on an unsecured basis, but frequently a borrower's credit rating is not strong enough to justify an unsecured loan. The most common types of collateral used for short-term credit are accounts receivable and inventories.

Financing through accounts receivable can be done either by pledging the receivables or by selling them outright, a process called factoring in the United States. When a receivable is pledged, the borrower retains the risk that the person or firm that owes the receivable will not pay. This risk is typically passed on to the lender when factoring is involved.

When loans are secured by inventory, the lender takes title to them. He may or may not take physical possession of them. Under a field warehousing arrangement, the inventory is under the physical control of a warehouse company, which releases the inventory only on order from the lending institution. Canned goods, lumber, steel, coal, and other standardized products are the types of goods usually covered in field warehouse arrangements.

INTERMEDIATE-TERM FINANCING

Whereas short-term loans are repaid in a period of weeks or months, intermediate-term loans are scheduled for repayment in 1 to 15 years. Obligations due in 15 or more years are thought of as long-term debt. The major forms of intermediate-term financing include (1) term loans, (2) conditional sales contracts, and (3) lease financing.

TERM LOANS

A term loan is a business credit with a maturity of more than 1 year but less than 15 years. Usually the term loan is retired by systematic repayments (amortization payments) over its life. It may be secured by a chattel mortgage on equipment, but larger, stronger companies are able to borrow on an unsecured basis. Commercial banks and life insurance companies are the principal suppliers of term loans. The interest cost of term loans varies with the size of the loan and the strength of the borrower.

Term loans involve more risk to the lender than do short-term loans. The lending institution's funds are tied up for a long period, and during this time the borrower's situation can change markedly. To protect themselves, lenders often include in the loan agreement stipulations that the borrowing company maintain its current liquidity ratio at a specified level, limit its acquisitions of fixed assets, keep its debt ratio below a stated amount, and in general follow policies that are acceptable to the lending institution.

CONDITIONAL SALES CONTRACTS

Conditional sales contracts represent a common method of obtaining equipment by agreeing to pay for it in installments over a period of up to five years. The seller of the equipment continues to hold title to the equipment until payment has been completed.

LEASE FINANCING

It is not necessary to purchase assets in order to use them. Railroad and airline companies in the United States, for instance, have acquired much of their equipment by leasing it. Whether leasing is advantageous depends—aside from tax advantages—on the firm's access to funds. Leasing provides an alternative method of financing. A lease contract, however, being a fixed obligation, is similar to debt and uses some of the firm's debt-carrying ability. It is generally advantageous for a

When equipment, such as aircraft, is prohibitively expensive to purchase, companies often turn to leasing, financing, and other options. Bloomberg/Getty Images

87

firm to own its land and buildings because their value is likely to increase, but the same possibility of appreciation does not apply to equipment.

The statement is frequently made that leasing involves higher interest rates than other forms of financing, but this need not always be true. Much depends on the firm's standing as a credit risk. Moreover, it is difficult to separate the cash costs of leasing from the other services that may be embodied in a leasing contract. If the leasing company can perform nonfinancial services (such as maintenance of the equipment) at a lower cost than the lessee or someone else could perform them, the effective cost of leasing may be lower than other financing methods.

Although leasing involves fixed charges, it enables a firm to present lower debt-to-asset ratios in its financial statements. Many lenders, in examining financial statements, give less weight to a lease obligation than to a loan obligation.

CHAPTER EIGHT

BUSINESS FINANCE: THE LONG TERM

Long-term capital may be raised either through borrowing or by the issuance of stock. Long-term borrowing is done by selling bonds, which are promissory notes that obligate the firm to pay interest at specific times. Secured bondholders have prior claim on the firm's assets. If the company goes out of business, the bondholders are entitled to be paid the face value of their holdings plus interest. Stockholders, on the other hand, have no more than a residual claim on the company; they are entitled to a share of the profits, if there are any, but it is the prerogative of the board of directors to decide whether a dividend will be paid and how large it will be.

Long-term financing involves the choice between debt (bonds) and equity (stocks). Each firm chooses its own capital structure, seeking the combination of debt and equity that will minimize the costs of raising capital. As conditions in the capital market vary (for instance, changes in interest rates, the availability of funds, and the relative costs of alternative methods of financing), the firm's desired capital structure will change correspondingly.

The larger the proportion of debt in the capital structure (leverage), the higher will be the returns to equity. This is because bondholders do not share in the profits. The difficulty with this, of course, is that a high proportion of debt increases a firm's fixed costs and increases the degree of fluctuation in the returns to equity for any given degree of fluctuation in the level of sales. If used successfully, leverage increases the returns to owners, but it decreases the returns to owners when it is used unsuccessfully. Indeed, if leverage is unsuccessful, the result may be the bankruptcy of the firm.

LONG-TERM DEBT

There are various forms of long-term debt. A mortgage bond is one secured by a lien on fixed assets such as plant and equipment. A debenture is a bond not secured by specific assets but accepted by investors because the firm has a high credit standing or obligates itself to follow policies that ensure a high rate of earnings. A still more junior lien is the subordinated debenture, which is secondary (in terms of ability to reclaim capital in the event of a business liquidation) to all other debentures and specifically to short-term bank loans.

Periods of relatively stable sales and earnings encourage the use of long-term debt. Other conditions that favour the use of long-term debt include large profit margins (they make additional leverage advantageous to the stockholders), an expected increase in profits or price levels, a low debt ratio, a price-earnings ratio that is low in relation to interest rates, and bond indentures that do not impose heavy restrictions on management.

STOCK

Equity financing is done with common and preferred stock. While both forms of stock represent shares of ownership in a company, preferred stock usually has priority over common stock with respect to earnings and claims on assets in the event of liquidation. Preferred stock is usually cumulative—that is, the omission of dividends in one or more years creates an accumulated claim that must be paid to holders of preferred shares. The dividends on preferred stock are usually fixed at a specific percentage of face value. A company issuing preferred stock gains the advantages of limited dividends and no maturity—that is, the advantages of selling bonds but without the restrictions of bonds. Companies sell preferred stock when they seek more leverage but wish to avoid the fixed charges of debt. The advantages of preferred stock will be reinforced if a company's debt ratio is already high and if common stock financing is relatively expensive.

If a bond or preferred stock issue was sold when interest rates were higher than at present, it may be profitable to call the old issue and refund it with a new, lower-cost issue. This depends on how the immediate costs and premiums that must be paid compare with the annual savings that can be obtained.

EARNINGS AND DIVIDEND POLICIES

The size and frequency of dividend payments are critical issues in company policy. Dividend policy affects the financial structure, the flow of funds, corporate liquidity, stock prices, and the morale of stockholders. Some stockholders prefer receiving maximum current returns on their investment, while others prefer reinvestment of earnings so that the company's capital will increase. If

Coca-Cola is among those companies that can pay high dividends because of stable earnings. Barry Williams/Getty Images

earnings are paid out as dividends, however, they cannot be used for company expansion (which thereby diminishes the company's long-term prospects). Many companies have opted to pay no regular dividend to shareholders, choosing instead to pursue strategies that increase the value of the stock.

Companies tend to reinvest their earnings more when there are chances for profitable expansion. Thus, at times when profits are high, the amounts reinvested are greater and dividends are smaller. For similar reasons, reinvestment is likely to decrease when profits decline, and dividends are likely to increase.

Companies having relatively stable earnings over a period of years tend to pay high dividends. Well-established large firms are likely to pay higher-than-average dividends because they have better access to capital markets and are not as likely to depend on internal financing. A firm with a strong cash or liquidity position is also likely to pay higher dividends. A firm with heavy indebtedness, however, has implicitly committed itself to paying relatively low dividends: earnings must be retained to service the debt. There can be advantages to this approach. If, for example, the directors of a company are concerned with maintaining control of it, they may retain earnings so that they can finance expansion without having to issue stock to outside investors. Some companies favour a stable dividend policy rather than allowing dividends to fluctuate with earnings. The dividend rate will then be lower when profits are high and higher when profits are temporarily in decline. Companies whose stock is closely held by a few high-income stockholders are likely to pay lower dividends in order to lower the stockholders' individual income taxes.

STOCK OPTION

A stock option is a contractual agreement enabling the holder to buy or sell a security at a designated price for a specified period of time, unaffected by movements in its market price during the period. Put and call options, purchased both for speculative and hedging reasons, are made by persons anticipating changes in stock prices. A put gives its holder an option to sell, or put, shares to the other party at a fixed put price even though the market price declines; a call, on the other hand, gives the holder an option to buy, or call for, shares at a fixed call price notwithstanding a market rise.

Another form of option, a stock purchase warrant, entitles its owner to buy shares of a common stock at a specified price (the exercise price of the warrant). Warrants are often issued with senior securities (preferred stocks and bonds) as "sweeteners" to increase their salability. They may also be issued directly as part of the compensation for underwriters of new issues and other promoters in the establishment of a new business.

The stock rights option gives a stockholder the choice of (1) buying additional stock at a price below the current market price for a specified period of time, usually briefer than the life span of stock purchase warrants, or (2) selling the rights on the market. They are the customary way of implementing the stockholder's preemptive right to subscribe to whatever additional stock is issued in order to maintain his proportionate equity in the corporation and its control.

American corporations frequently issue employee stock options as a form of incentive compensation for their executives. The underlying theory is that an option constitutes an incentive to do what will improve the company's fortunes and thus raise the value of its stock.

In Europe, company financing historically relied heavily on internal sources. This was because many companies were owned by families and also because a highly developed capital market was lacking. In the less-developed countries today, firms rely heavily on internal financing, but they also tend to make more use of short-term bank loans, microcredit, and other forms of short-term financing than is typical in other countries.

CONVERTIBLE BONDS AND STOCK WARRANTS

Companies sometimes issue bonds or preferred stock that give holders the option of converting them into common stock or of purchasing stock at favourable prices. Convertible bonds carry the option of conversion into common stock at a specified price during a particular period. Stock purchase warrants are given with bonds or preferred stock as an inducement to the investor because they permit the purchase of the company's common stock at a stated price at any time. Such option privileges make it easier for small companies to sell bonds or preferred stock. They help large companies to float new issues on more favourable terms than they could otherwise obtain. When bondholders exercise conversion rights, the company's debt ratio is reduced because bonds are replaced by stock. The exercise of stock warrants, on the other hand, brings additional funds into the company but leaves the existing debt or preferred stock on the books. Option privileges also permit a company to sell new stock at more favourable prices than those prevailing at the time of issue, since the prices stated on the options are higher. Stock purchase warrants are

A trader places an order in the S&P 500 options pit at the Chicago Board Options Exchange. Brian Kersey/Getty Images

most popular, therefore, at times when stock prices are expected to have an upward trend.

MERGERS AND REORGANIZATION

Companies often grow by combining with other companies. One company may purchase all or part of another; two companies may merge by exchanging shares; or a wholly new company may be formed through consolidation of the old companies. From the financial manager's viewpoint, this kind of expansion is like any other investment decision: the acquisition should be made if it increases the acquiring firm's net present value as reflected in the price of its stock.

The most important term that must be negotiated in a combination is the price the acquiring firm will pay for the assets it takes over. Present earnings, expected future earnings, and the effects of the merger on the rate of earnings growth of the surviving firm are perhaps the most important determinants of the price that will be paid. Current market prices are the second most important determinant of prices in mergers; depending on whether asset values are indicative of the earning power of the acquired firm, book values may exert an important influence on the terms of the merger. Other, nonmeasurable, factors are sometimes the overriding determinant in bringing companies together. Synergistic effects (wherein the net result is greater than the combined value of the individual components) may be attractive enough to warrant paying a price that is higher than earnings and asset values would indicate.

The basic requirements for a successful merger are that it fit into a soundly conceived long-range plan and that the performance of the resulting firm be superior to those attainable by the previous companies independently. In the heady environment of a rising stock market, mergers have often been motivated by superficial financial aims. Companies with stock selling at a high price relative to earnings have found it advantageous to merge with companies having a lower price-earnings ratio. This enables them to increase their earnings per share and thus appeal to investors who purchase stock on the basis of earnings.

Some mergers, particularly those of conglomerates, which bring together firms in unrelated fields, owe their

Jeff Smisek (left), CEO of Continental Airlines, and Glenn Tilton, CEO of United Airlines' parent company, UAL Corp., on May 3, 2010 at the announcement of the merger of their airlines. Bloomberg/Getty Images

success to economies of management that developed throughout the 20th century. New strategies emphasized the importance of general managerial functions (planning, control, organization, and information management) and other top-level managerial tasks (research, finance, legal services, and technology). These changes reduced the costs of managing large, diversified firms and prompted an increase in mergers and acquisitions among corporations around the world.

When a merger occurs, one firm disappears. Alternatively, one firm may buy all (or a majority) of the voting stock of another and then run that company as an operating subsidiary. The acquiring firm is then called a holding company. There are several advantages in the holding company: it can control the acquired firm with a smaller investment than would be required in a merger; each firm remains a separate legal entity, and the obligations of one are separate from those of the other; and, finally, stockholder approval is not necessary—as it is in the case of a merger. There are also disadvantages to holding companies, including the possibility of multiple taxation and the danger that the high rate of leverage will amplify the earnings fluctuations (be they losses or gains) of the operating companies.

When a firm cannot operate profitably, the owners may seek to reorganize it. The first question to be answered is whether the firm might not be better off by ceasing to do business. If the decision is made that the firm is to survive, it must be put through the process of reorganization. Legal procedures are always costly, especially in the case of business failure, and both the debtor and the creditors are frequently better off settling matters on an informal basis rather than through the courts. The informal procedures used in reorganization are (1) extension, which postpones the settlement of outstanding debt, and (2) composition, which reduces the amount owed.

If voluntary settlement through extension or composition is not possible, the matter must be taken to court. If the court decides on reorganization rather than liquidation, it appoints a trustee to control the firm and to prepare a formal plan of reorganization. The plan must meet standards of fairness and feasibility: the concept of fairness involves the appropriate distribution of proceeds to each claimant, while the test of feasibility relates to the ability of the new enterprise to carry the fixed charges resulting from the reorganization plan.

CONCLUSION

Banks are institutions that deal in money and its substitutes and provide a range of other financial services, though their principal activity consists of borrowing and lending. Some banks, known as central banks, have the power to create money. Among commercial banks, most accept deposits from the public and make various kinds of personal and business loans, while some deal primarily with business clients and perform services such as underwriting issues of stock and corporate bonds, advising on mergers and acquisitions, managing investment funds, and selling various types of securities and insurance. Until the repeal in 1999 of relevant provisions of the Depression-era Glass-Steagall Act (1933), banks in the United States had not been permitted to deal in securities or insurance. Banks make profits from interest charges on loans, returns on their own securities investments, and commissions for services rendered.

Central banks provide financial services to governments and act as lenders of last resort to commercial banks. In cooperation with governments they also formulate and implement monetary and credit policies, usually with the aim of controlling inflation, maintaining economic growth, reducing unemployment, and ensuring the soundness of the commercial banking sector.

The practices through which businesses raise and manage funds are known as business finance. To gauge the financial requirements of a firm in the short term, managers employ a variety of tools, including ratio analysis (e.g., analysis of the ratio of current assets to current liabilities), profit planning, financial forecasting, and budgeting. Accounts receivable and inventory control are also important elements of short-term finance. When needed, businesses may obtain short- and intermediate-term financing through trade credits from suppliers, commercial bank loans, commercial paper, secured loans, installment sales contracts, and leases. Long-term capital may be raised in the form of debt (bonds) or equity (stock), the relative advantages of which must be weighed by corporate financial officers. While the sale of bonds offers a firm leverage (in this case, the potential to increase profits without increasing equity, or the total claims of shareholders), the issuance of stock creates no new fixed costs, such as regular interest payments to bondholders. Other strategies for increasing long-term financial growth are mergers, acquisitions, and reorganizations, each of which poses unique and complex challenges.

GLOSSARY

asset The entire property of a person, association, corporation, or estate applicable or subject to the payment of debts.

base money The amount of money that is held by the public and deposited with reserve banks

bullion Un-coined gold or silver in bars or ingots.

clearinghouse An establishment maintained by banks for settling mutual claims and accounts.

commercial bank A bank organized chiefly to handle the everyday financial transactions of businesses (as through demand deposit accounts and short-term commercial loans).

credit union A cooperative association that makes small loans to its members at low interest rates and offers other banking services (as savings and checking accounts).

discount rate Interest rate charged by a central bank for loans of reserve funds to commercial banks and other financial intermediaries.

equity The money value of a property or of an interest in a property in excess of claims or liens against it.

fiat money Money (as paper currency) not convertible into coin or specie of equivalent value.

hedge fund An investing group usually in the form of a limited partnership that employs speculative techniques in the hope of obtaining large capital gains.

inflation A continuing rise in the general price level usually attributed to an increase in the volume of money and credit relative to available goods and services.

insolvent Having liabilities in excess of a reasonable market value of assets held.

interest A charge for borrowed money, generally a percentage of the amount borrowed.

liability Something (such as the payment of money) for which a person or business is legally responsible.

liquidity The quality of being easily changed into money.

loan shark Someone who lends money to people at a very high rate of interest.

merchant bank A firm that originates, underwrites, and distributes new security issues of corporations and government agencies.

money market The trade in short-term negotiable instruments (as certificates of deposit or United States Treasury securities).

mutual fund An open-end investment company that invests money of its shareholders in a usually diversified group of securities of other corporations.

savings and loan association A savings and home-financing institution that makes loans for the purchase of private housing, home improvements, and new construction.

treasury note A government security, usually marketable, with maturity ranging from one to five years.

usury The practice of lending money at an unreasonably high rate of interest.

venture capital Capital (as retained corporate earnings or individual savings) invested or available for investment in the ownership element of new or fresh enterprise.

BIBLIOGRAPHY

THE DEVELOPMENT OF BANKING SYSTEMS

The history of banking in Great Britain from its beginnings in the mid-18th century to the start of World War II is discussed in Stanley Chapman, *The Rise of Merchant Banking* (1984, reissued 2006). Developments in the United States are covered in Howard Bodenhorn, *State Banking in Early America: A New Economic History* (2003). Other regional studies include Charles P. Kindleberger, *A Financial History of Western Europe*, 2nd ed. (1993).

The origins of central banking are discussed in Vera C. Smith, *The Rationale of Central Banking* (1936, reprinted in 1990 as *The Rationale of Central Banking and the Free Banking Alternative*). Rondo E. Cameron et al., *Banking in the Early Stages of Industrialization: A Study in Comparative Economic History* (1967), is a classic treatment of banking and economic development.

THE BUSINESS OF BANKING AND BANK REGULATION

Modern commercial banking practices are addressed by Edward W. Reed and Edward K. Gill, *Commercial Banking*, 4th ed. (1989), a textbook. Shelagh A. Heffernan, *Modern Banking* (2005), covers theory and practice in banking; and James R. Barth, Gerard Caprio, and Ross Levine, *Rethinking Bank Regulation: Till Angels Govern* (2006), assesses the effects of regulatory policies on banks around the world.

WORLD BANK

A comprehensive review of bank operations is Devesh Kapur, John P. Lewis, and Richard Webb, *The World Bank: Its First Half Century*, 2 vol. (1997). Katherine Marshall, *The World Bank* (2008), provides a much briefer overview. An incisive analysis of the inner workings of the World Bank Group and its interests is Susan George and Fabrizio Sabelli, *Faith and Credit: The World Bank's Secular Empire* (1994). Discussions of IBRD reforms include Kevin Danaher (ed.), *Fifty Years Is Enough: The Case Against the World Bank and the International Monetary Fund* (1994); Michel Chossudovsky, *The Globalisation of Poverty: Impacts of IMF and World Bank Reforms* (1997); and Bruce Rich, *Mortgaging the Earth: The World Bank, Environmental Impoverishment, and the Crisis of Development* (1994).

BUSINESS FINANCE

Comprehensive introductions to the theory of business finance include J. Fred Weston, Scott Besley, and Eugene F. Brigham, *Essentials of Managerial Finance*, 11th ed. (1996); and James C. Van Horne, *Financial Management and Policy*, 12th ed. (2002). Practical guides to balance-sheet analysis and finance for the layman are Eugene F. Brigham and Joel F. Houston, *Fundamentals of Financial Management*, 12th ed. (2009); and Gerald I. White, Ashwinpaul C. Sondhi, and Dov Fried, *The Analysis and Use of Financial Statements*, 3rd ed. (2003).

INDEX

D